I0783503

Romeo and Juliet

William Shakespeare

Living Popups illustrated and
AUGMENTED REALITY enabled

Augmented reality popups featuring animation
by Living Popups and the voices of:

Shakespeare *Tom Payne*
Gregory *Eric McCormack*
Samson *Sacha Dhawan*
Abraham *Steven Weber*
Balthasar *Arnold Oceng*

Ruby *Kate Walsh*

- Get the app -
Search **LP Bookspace** on iOS and Android

WELCOME

Welcome to the Living Popups illustrated and augmented reality enabled printing of *Romeo and Juliet* by **William Shakespeare**.

Published in the 1590's and set in Verona Italy, the play focuses on two star-crossed lovers whose deaths ultimately reconcile their feuding families.

The text is formatted as a play with the character name followed by their lines. Shakespeare was quite spare in his stage direction but those instructions to the actors that do appear are printed in italics. A frequent one is:

> *Exeunt*
> **ˈeksēˌənt / verb** - A stage direction in a printed play to indicate that a group of characters leave the stage.

In this version, at key points in the text, AR enabled illustrations serve as targets that come to life on a mobile device running the Living Popups AR Reading Companion App*. The popups give context and additional background to help you understand the story and give important and interesting context.

At the start of each chapter, characters from the story will give you insights into what is coming and at the end of each chapter they will challenge you with an interactive question.

Simply start the app, point the camera at the illustrations and let the characters from *Romeo and Juliet* take it from there!

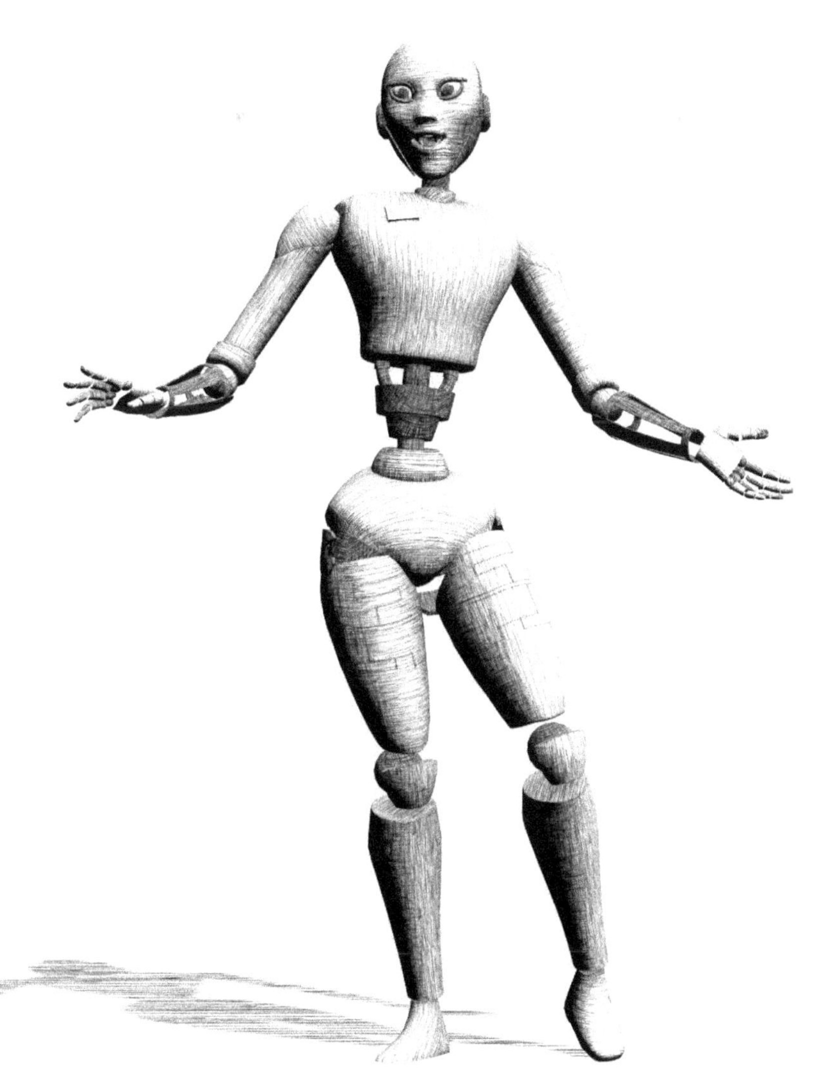

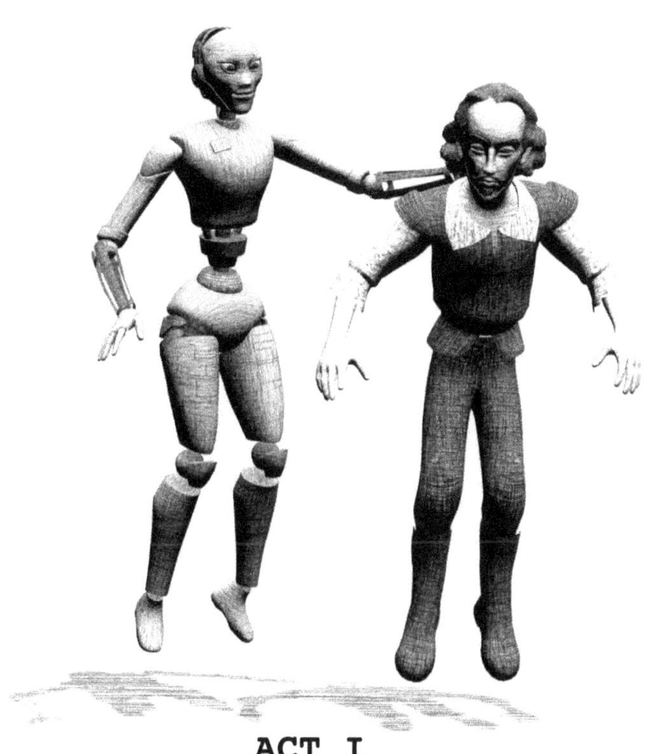

ACT I

PROLOGUE

*Two households, both alike in dignity, In fair
Verona, where we lay our scene, From ancient
grudge break to new mutiny, Where civil blood
makes civil hands unclean. From forth the fatal
loins of these two foes A pair of star-cross'd
lovers take their life; Whose misadventured
piteous overthrows Do with their death bury their
parents' strife. The fearful passage of their
death-mark'd love, And the continuance of their
parents' rage, Which, but their children's end,
nought could remove, Is now the two hours' traffic
of our stage; The which if you with patient ears
attend, What here shall miss, our toil shall
strive to mend.*

SCENE 1. VERONA. A PUBLIC PLACE.

*Enter SAMPSON and GREGORY, of the house of
Capulet, armed with swords and bucklers*

SAMPSON

Gregory, o' my word, we'll not carry coals.

GREGORY

No, for then we should be colliers.

SAMPSON

I mean, an we be in choler, we'll draw.

GREGORY

Ay, while you live, draw your neck out o'
the collar.

SAMPSON

I strike quickly, being moved.

GREGORY

But thou art not quickly moved to strike.

SAMPSON

A dog of the house of Montague moves me.

GREGORY

To move is to stir; and to be valiant is to
stand: therefore, if thou art moved, thou
runn'st away.

SAMPSON

A dog of that house shall move me to stand:
I will take the wall of any man or maid of
Montague's.

GREGORY

That shows thee a weak slave; for the
weakest goes to the wall.

SAMPSON

True; and therefore women, being the weaker
vessels, are ever thrust to the wall:
therefore I will push Montague's men from
the wall, and thrust his maids to the wall.

GREGORY

The quarrel is between our masters and us
their men.

SAMPSON

'Tis all one, I will show myself a tyrant:
when I have fought with the men, I will be
cruel with the maids, and cut off their
heads.

GREGORY

The heads of the maids?

SAMPSON

Ay, the heads of the maids, or their
maidenheads; take it in what sense thou
wilt.

GREGORY

They must take it in sense that feel it.

SAMPSON

Me they shall feel while I am able to
stand: and 'tis known I am a pretty piece
of flesh.

GREGORY

'Tis well thou art not fish; if thou hadst,
thou hadst been poor John. Draw thy tool!
here comes two of the house of the
Montagues.

SAMPSON

My naked weapon is out: quarrel, I will
back thee.

GREGORY

How! turn thy back and run?

SAMPSON

Fear me not.

GREGORY

No, marry; I fear thee!

SAMPSON

Let us take the law of our sides; let them begin.

GREGORY

I will frown as I pass by, and let them take it as they list.

SAMPSON

Nay, as they dare. I will bite my thumb at them; which is a disgrace to them, if they bear it.

Enter ABRAHAM and BALTHASAR

ABRAHAM

Do you bite your thumb at us, sir?

SAMPSON

I do bite my thumb, sir.

ABRAHAM

Do you bite your thumb at us, sir?

SAMPSON

(Aside to GREGORY)
Is the law of our side, if I say ay?

GREGORY

No.

SAMPSON

No, sir, I do not bite my thumb at you, sir, but I bite my thumb, sir.

GREGORY

>   Do you quarrel, sir?

ABRAHAM

>   Quarrel sir! no, sir.

SAMPSON

>   If you do, sir, I am for you: I serve as
>   good a man as you.

ABRAHAM

>   No better.

SAMPSON

>   Well, sir.

GREGORY

>   Say 'better:' here comes one of my master's
>   kinsmen.

SAMPSON

>   Yes, better, sir.

ABRAHAM

>   You lie.

SAMPSON

>   Draw, if you be men. Gregory, remember thy
>   swashing blow. They fight

Enter BENVOLIO

BENVOLIO

>   Part, fools! Put up your swords; you know
>   not what you do. Beats down their swords

Enter TYBALT

TYBALT

> What, art thou drawn among these heartless hinds? Turn thee, Benvolio, look upon thy death.

BENVOLIO

> I do but keep the peace: put up thy sword, Or manage it to part these men with me.

TYBALT

> What, drawn, and talk of peace! I hate the word, As I hate hell, all Montagues, and thee: Have at thee, coward! They fightEnter, several of both houses, who join the fray; then enter Citizens, with clubsFirst Citizen Clubs, bills, and partisans! strike! beat them down! Down with the Capulets! down with the Montagues!

Enter CAPULET in his gown, and LADY CAPULET

CAPULET

> What noise is this? Give me my long sword, ho!

LADY CAPULET

> A crutch, a crutch! why call you for a sword?

CAPULET

> My sword, I say! Old Montague is come, And flourishes his blade in spite of me.

Enter MONTEGUE and LADY MONTEGUE

MONTAGUE

> Thou villain Capulet,--Hold me not, let me go.

LADY MONTAGUE

Thou shalt not stir a foot to seek a foe.

Enter PRINCE, with Attendants

PRINCE

Rebellious subjects, enemies to peace,
Profaners of this neighbour-stained steel,—
Will they not hear? What, ho! you men, you
beasts, That quench the fire of your
pernicious rage With purple fountains
issuing from your veins, On pain of
torture, from those bloody hands Throw your
mistemper'd weapons to the ground, And hear
the sentence of your moved prince. Three
civil brawls, bred of an airy word, By
thee, old Capulet, and Montague, Have
thrice disturb'd the quiet of our streets,
And made Verona's ancient citizens Cast by
their grave beseeming ornaments, To wield
old partisans, in hands as old, Canker'd
with peace, to part your canker'd hate: If
ever you disturb our streets again, Your
lives shall pay the forfeit of the peace.
For this time, all the rest depart away:
You Capulet; shall go along with me: And,
Montague, come you this afternoon, To know
our further pleasure in this case, To old
Free-town, our common judgment-place. Once
more, on pain of death, all men depart.

*Exeunt all but MONTEGUE, LADY MONTEGUE, and
BENVOLIO*

MONTAGUE

Who set this ancient quarrel new abroach?
Speak, nephew, were you by when it began?

BENVOLIO

Here were the servants of your
adversary,And yours, close fighting ere I
did approach:I drew to part them: in the
instant came The fiery Tybalt, with his
sword prepared, Which, as he breathed
defiance to my ears,He swung about his head
and cut the winds, Who nothing hurt withal
hiss'd him in scorn: While we were
interchanging thrusts and blows, Came more
and more and fought on part and part,Till
the prince came, who parted either part.

LADY MONTAGUE

O, where is Romeo? saw you him to-day?
Right glad I am he was not at this fray.

BENVOLIO

Madam, an hour before the worshipp'd
sunPeer'd forth the golden window of the
east, A troubled mind drave me to walk
abroad; Where, underneath the grove of
sycamore That westward rooteth from the
city's side,So early walking did I see your
son Towards him I made, but he was ware of
me And stole into the covert of the wood:
I, measuring his affections by my own, That
most are busied when they're most alone,
Pursued my humour not pursuing his,And
gladly shunn'd who gladly fled from me.

MONTAGUE

Many a morning hath he there been seen,With
tears augmenting the fresh morning
dew.Adding to clouds more clouds with his
deep sighs;But all so soon as the all-
cheering sun Should in the furthest east
begin to draw The shady curtains from

Aurora's bed,Away from the light steals
home my heavy son,And private in his
chamber pens himself, Shuts up his windows,
locks far daylight outAnd makes himself an
artificial night:Black and portentous must
this humour prove, Unless good counsel may
the cause remove.

BENVOLIO

My noble uncle, do you know the cause?

MONTAGUE

I neither know it nor can learn of him.

BENVOLIO

Have you importuned him by any means?

MONTAGUE

Both by myself and many other friends: But
he, his own affections' counsellor, Is to
himself--I will not say how true--But to
himself so secret and so close,So far from
sounding and discovery,As is the bud bit
with an envious worm,Ere he can spread his
sweet leaves to the air,Or dedicate his
beauty to the sun.Could we but learn from
whence his sorrows grow.We would as
willingly give cure as know.

Enter ROMEO

BENVOLIO

See, where he comes: so please you, step
aside; I'll know his grievance, or be much
denied.

MONTAGUE

> I would thou wert so happy by thy stay, To
> hear true shrift. Come, madam, let's away.

Exeunt MONTEGUE and LADY MONTEGUE

BENVOLIO

> Good-morrow, cousin.

ROMEO

> Is the day so young?

BENVOLIO

> But new struck nine.

ROMEO

> Ay me! sad hours seem long. Was that my
> father that went hence so fast?

BENVOLIO

> It was. What sadness lengthens Romeo's
> hours?

ROMEO

> Not having that, which, having, makes them
> short.

BENVOLIO

> In love?

ROMEO

> Out--

BENVOLIO

> Of love?

ROMEO

> Out of her favour, where I am in love.

BENVOLIO

> Alas, that love, so gentle in his view,
> Should be so tyrannous and rough in proof!

ROMEO

> Alas, that love, whose view is muffled
> still, Should, without eyes, see pathways
> to his will! Where shall we dine? O me!
> What fray was here? Yet tell me not, for I
> have heard it all. Here's much to do with
> hate, but more with love. Why, then, O
> brawling love! O loving hate! O any thing,
> of nothing first create! O heavy lightness!
> serious vanity! Mis-shapen chaos of well-
> seeming forms! Feather of lead, bright
> smoke, cold fire, sick health! Still-waking
> sleep, that is not what it is! This love
> feel I, that feel no love in this. Dost
> thou not laugh?

BENVOLIO

> No, coz, I rather weep.

ROMEO

> Good heart, at what?

BENVOLIO

> At thy good heart's oppression.

ROMEO

> Why, such is love's transgression.
> Griefs of mine own lie heavy in my breast,
> Which thou wilt propagate, to have it prest
> With more of thine: this love that thou
> hast shown Doth add more grief to too much
> of mine own. Love is a smoke raised with
> the fume of sighs; Being purged, a fire
> sparkling in lovers' eyes; Being vex'd a

sea nourish'd with lovers' tears: What is
it else? a madness most discreet, A choking
gall and a preserving sweet. Farewell, my
coz.

BENVOLIO

Soft! I will go along; An if you leave me
so, you do me wrong.

ROMEO

Tut, I have lost myself; I am not here;
This is not Romeo, he's some other where.

BENVOLIO

Tell me in sadness, who is that you love.

ROMEO

What, shall I groan and tell thee?

BENVOLIO

Groan! why, no. But sadly tell me who.

ROMEO

Bid a sick man in sadness make his will:
Ah, word ill urged to one that is so ill!
In sadness, cousin, I do love a woman.

BENVOLIO

I aim'd so near, when I supposed you loved.

ROMEO

A right good mark-man! And she's fair I
love.

BENVOLIO

A right fair mark, fair coz, is soonest
hit.

ROMEO

Well, in that hit you miss: she'll not be hit With Cupid's arrow; she hath Dian's wit; And, in strong proof of chastity well arm'd, From love's weak childish bow she lives unharm'd. She will not stay the siege of loving terms, Nor bide the encounter of assailing eyes, Nor ope her lap to saint-seducing gold: O, she is rich in beauty, only poor, That when she dies with beauty dies her store.

BENVOLIO

Then she hath sworn that she will still live chaste?

ROMEO

She hath, and in that sparing makes huge waste, For beauty starved with her severity Cuts beauty off from all posterity. She is too fair, too wise, wisely too fair, To merit bliss by making me despair: She hath forsworn to love, and in that vow Do I live dead that live to tell it now.

BENVOLIO

Be ruled by me, forget to think of her.

ROMEO

O, teach me how I should forget to think.

BENVOLIO

By giving liberty unto thine eyes; Examine other beauties.

ROMEO

'Tis the way To call hers exquisite, in question more: These happy masks that kiss

fair ladies' brows Being black put us in
mind they hide the fair; He that is
strucken blind cannot forget The precious
treasure of his eyesight lost: Show me a
mistress that is passing fair, What doth
her beauty serve, but as a note Where I may
read who pass'd that passing fair?
Farewell: thou canst not teach me to
forget.

BENVOLIO

I'll pay that doctrine, or else die in
debt.

SCENE 2. A STREET.

Enter CAPULET, PARIS, and SERVANT

CAPULET

> But Montague is bound as well as I, In
> penalty alike; and 'tis not hard, I think,
> For men so old as we to keep the peace.

PARIS

> Of honourable reckoning are you both; And
> pity 'tis you lived at odds so long. But
> now, my lord, what say you to my suit?

CAPULET

But saying o'er what I have said before: My
child is yet a stranger in the world; She
hath not seen the change of fourteen years,
Let two more summers wither in their pride,
Ere we may think her ripe to be a bride.

PARIS

Younger than she are happy mothers made.

CAPULET

And too soon marr'd are those so early
made. The earth hath swallow'd all my hopes
but she, She is the hopeful lady of my
earth: But woo her, gentle Paris, get her
heart, My will to her consent is but a
part; An she agree, within her scope of
choice Lies my consent and fair according
voice. This night I hold an old accustom'd
feast, Whereto I have invited many a guest,
Such as I love; and you, among the store,
One more, most welcome, makes my number
more. At my poor house look to behold this
night Earth-treading stars that make dark
heaven light: Such comfort as do lusty
young men feel When well-apparell'd April
on the heel Of limping winter treads, even
such delight Among fresh female buds shall
you this night Inherit at my house; hear
all, all see, And like her most whose merit
most shall be: Which on more view, of many
mine being one May stand in number, though
in reckoning none, Come, go with me.
(To Servant, giving a paper)
Go, sirrah, trudge about Through fair
Verona; find those persons out Whose names
are written there, and to them say, My
house and welcome on their pleasure stay.

Exeunt CAPULET and PARIS

CAPULET

Servant Find them out whose names are
written here! It is written, that the
shoemaker should meddle with his yard, and
the tailor with his last, the fisher with
his pencil, and the painter with his nets;
but I am sent to find those persons whose
names are here writ, and can never find what
names the writing person hath here writ. I
must to the learned.--In good time.

Enter BENVOLIO and ROMEO

BENVOLIO

Tut, man, one fire burns out another's
burning, One pain is lessen'd by another's
anguish; Turn giddy, and be holp by
backward turning; One desperate grief cures
with another's languish: Take thou some new
infection to thy eye, And the rank poison
of the old will die.

ROMEO

Your plaintain-leaf is excellent for that.

BENVOLIO

For what, I pray thee?

ROMEO

For your broken shin.

BENVOLIO

Why, Romeo, art thou mad?

ROMEO

Not mad, but bound more than a mad-man is;

> Shut up in prison, kept without my food,
> Whipp'd and tormented and--God-den, good
> fellow.

SERVANT

> God gi' god-den. I pray, sir, can you read?

ROMEO

> Ay, mine own fortune in my misery.

SERVANT

> Perhaps you have learned it without book:
> but, I pray, can you read any thing you
> see?

ROMEO

> Ay, if I know the letters and the language.

SERVANT

> Ye say honestly: rest you merry!

ROMEO

> Stay, fellow; I can read.
> (Reads)
> 'Signior Martino and his wife and
> daughters; County Anselme and his beauteous
> sisters; the lady widow of Vitravio;
> Signior Placentio and his lovely nieces;
> Mercutio and his brother Valentine; mine
> uncle Capulet, his wife and daughters; my
> fair niece Rosaline; Livia; Signior
> Valentio and his cousin Tybalt, Lucio and
> the lively Helena.' A fair assembly:
> whither should they come?

SERVANT

> Up.

ROMEO

Whither?

SERVANT

To supper; to our house.

ROMEO

Whose house?

SERVANT

My master's.

ROMEO

Indeed, I should have ask'd you that
before.

SERVANT

Now I'll tell you without asking: my master
is the great rich Capulet; and if you be
not of the house of Montagues, I pray, come
and crush a cup of wine. Rest you merry!
Exit

BENVOLIO

At this same ancient feast of Capulet's
Sups the fair Rosaline whom thou so lovest,
With all the admired beauties of Verona: Go
thither; and, with unattainted eye, Compare
her face with some that I shall show, And I
will make thee think thy swan a crow.

ROMEO

When the devout religion of mine eye
Maintains such falsehood, then turn tears
to fires; And these, who often drown'd could
never die, Transparent heretics, be burnt
for liars! One fairer than my love! the

all-seeing sun Ne'er saw her match since
first the world begun.

BENVOLIO

Tut, you saw her fair, none else being by,
Herself poised with herself in either eye:
But in that crystal scales let there be
weigh'd Your lady's love against some other
maid That I will show you shining at this
feast, And she shall scant show well that
now shows best.

ROMEO

I'll go along, no such sight to be shown,
But to rejoice in splendor of mine own.

Exeunt

SCENE 3. A ROOM IN CAPULET'S HOUSE.

Enter LADY CAPULET and NURSE

LADY CAPULET

>Nurse, where's my daughter? call her forth
>to me.

NURSE

>Now, by my maidenhead, at twelve year old,
>I bade her come. What, lamb! what,
>ladybird! God forbid! Where's this girl?
>What, Juliet!

Enter JULIET

JULIET

How now! who calls?

NURSE

Your mother.

JULIET

Madam, I am here. What is your will?

LADY CAPULET

This is the matter:--Nurse, give leave
awhile, We must talk in secret:--nurse,
come back again; I have remember'd me,
thou's hear our counsel. Thou know'st my
daughter's of a pretty age.

NURSE

Faith, I can tell her age unto an hour.

LADY CAPULET

She's not fourteen.

NURSE

I'll lay fourteen of my teeth,— And yet, to
my teeth be it spoken, I have but four— She
is not fourteen. How long is it now To
Lammas-tide?

LADY CAPULET

A fortnight and odd days.

NURSE

Even or odd, of all days in the year, Come
Lammas-eve at night shall she be fourteen.
Susan and she--God rest all Christian
souls!— Were of an age: well, Susan is with

God; She was too good for me: but, as I
said, On Lammas-eve at night shall she be
fourteen; That shall she, marry; I remember
it well. 'Tis since the earthquake now
eleven years; And she was wean'd,--I never
shall forget it,— Of all the days of the
year, upon that day: For I had then laid
wormwood to my dug, Sitting in the sun
under the dove-house wall; My lord and you
were then at Mantua:— Nay, I do bear a
brain:--but, as I said, When it did taste
the wormwood on the nipple Of my dug and
felt it bitter, pretty fool, To see it
tetchy and fall out with the dug! Shake
quoth the dove-house: 'twas no need, I
trow, To bid me trudge: And since that time
it is eleven years; For then she could
stand alone; nay, by the rood, She could
have run and waddled all about; For even
the day before, she broke her brow: And
then my husband--God be with his soul! A'
was a merry man--took up the child: 'Yea,'
quoth he, 'dost thou fall upon thy face?
Thou wilt fall backward when thou hast more
wit; Wilt thou not, Jule?' and, by my
holidame, The pretty wretch left crying and
said 'Ay.' To see, now, how a jest shall
come about! I warrant, an I should live a
thousand years, I never should forget it:
'Wilt thou not, Jule?' quoth he; And,
pretty fool, it stinted and said 'Ay.'

LADY CAPULET

Enough of this; I pray thee, hold thy
peace.

NURSE

Yes, madam: yet I cannot choose but laugh,

To think it should leave crying and say
'Ay.' And yet, I warrant, it had upon its
brow A bump as big as a young cockerel's
stone; A parlous knock; and it cried
bitterly: 'Yea,' quoth my husband,'fall'st
upon thy face? Thou wilt fall backward when
thou comest to age; Wilt thou not, Jule?'
it stinted and said 'Ay.'

JULIET

And stint thou too, I pray thee, nurse, say
I.

NURSE

Peace, I have done. God mark thee to his
grace! Thou wast the prettiest babe that
e'er I nursed: An I might live to see thee
married once, I have my wish.

LADY CAPULET

Marry, that 'marry' is the very theme I
came to talk of. Tell me, daughter Juliet,
How stands your disposition to be married?

JULIET

It is an honour that I dream not of.

NURSE

An honour! were not I thine only nurse, I
would say thou hadst suck'd wisdom from thy
teat.

LADY CAPULET

Well, think of marriage now; younger than
you, Here in Verona, ladies of esteem, Are
made already mothers: by my count, I was
your mother much upon these years That you

are now a maid. Thus then in brief: The
valiant Paris seeks you for his love.

NURSE

A man, young lady! lady, such a man As all
the world--why, he's a man of wax.

LADY CAPULET

Verona's summer hath not such a flower.

NURSE

Nay, he's a flower; in faith, a very flower.

LADY CAPULET

What say you? can you love the gentleman?
This night you shall behold him at our
feast; Read o'er the volume of young Paris'
face, And find delight writ there with
beauty's pen; Examine every married
lineament, And see how one another lends
content And what obscured in this fair
volume lies Find written in the margent of
his eyes. This precious book of love, this
unbound lover, To beautify him, only lacks
a cover: The fish lives in the sea, and 'tis
much pride For fair without the fair within
to hide: That book in many's eyes doth
share the glory, That in gold clasps locks
in the golden story; So shall you share all
that he doth possess, By having him, making
yourself no less.

NURSE

No less! nay, bigger; women grow by men.

LADY CAPULET

Speak briefly, can you like of Paris' love?

JULIET

> I'll look to like, if looking liking move:
> But no more deep will I endart mine eye
> Than your consent gives strength to make it
> fly.

Enter a SERVANT

SERVANT

> Madam, the guests are come, supper served
> up, you called, my young lady asked for,
> the nurse cursed in the pantry, and every
> thing in extremity. I must hence to wait; I
> beseech you, follow straight.

LADY CAPULET

> We follow thee.

Exit SERVANT

JULIET, the county stays.

NURSE

> Go, girl, seek happy nights to happy days.

Exeunt

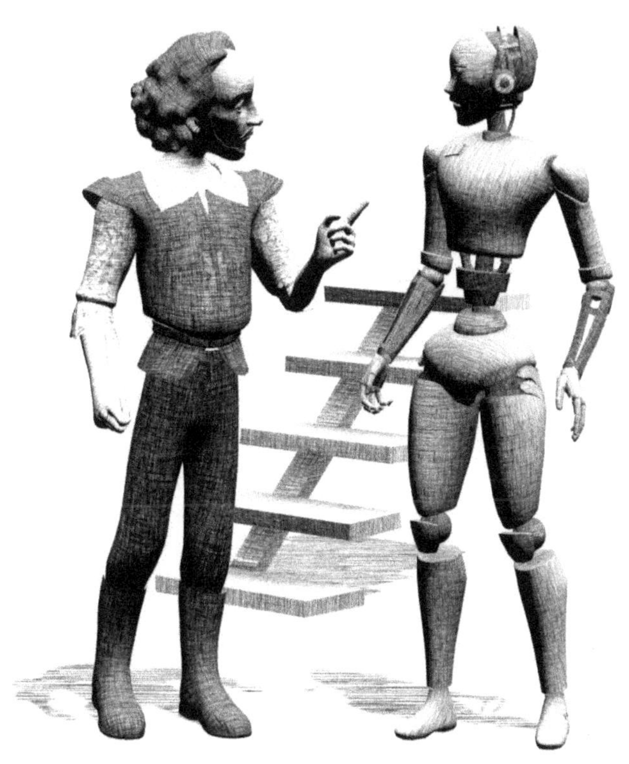

SCENE 4. A STREET.

Enter ROMEO, MERCUTIO, BENVOLIO, with five or six
Maskers, Torch-bearers, and others

ROMEO

> What, shall this speech be spoke for our
> excuse? Or shall we on without a apology?

BENVOLIO

> The date is out of such prolixity: We'll
> have no Cupid hoodwink'd with a scarf,
> Bearing a Tartar's painted bow of lath,
> Scaring the ladies like a crow-keeper; Nor

no without-book prologue, faintly spoke
After the prompter, for our entrance: But
let them measure us by what they will;
We'll measure them a measure, and be gone.

ROMEO

Give me a torch: I am not for this ambling;
Being but heavy, I will bear the light.

MERCUTIO

Nay, gentle Romeo, we must have you dance.

ROMEO

Not I, believe me: you have dancing shoes
With nimble soles: I have a soul of lead So
stakes me to the ground I cannot move.

MERCUTIO

You are a lover; borrow Cupid's wings, And
soar with them above a common bound.

ROMEO

I am too sore enpierced with his shaft To
soar with his light feathers, and so bound,
I cannot bound a pitch above dull woe:
Under love's heavy burden do I sink.

MERCUTIO

And, to sink in it, should you burden love;
Too great oppression for a tender thing.

ROMEO

Is love a tender thing? it is too rough,
Too rude, too boisterous, and it pricks
like thorn.

MERCUTIO

If love be rough with you, be rough with

love; Prick love for pricking, and you beat
love down. Give me a case to put my visage
in: A visor for a visor! what care I What
curious eye doth quote deformities? Here
are the beetle brows shall blush for me.

BENVOLIO

Come, knock and enter; and no sooner in,
But every man betake him to his legs.

ROMEO

A torch for me: let wantons light of heart
Tickle the senseless rushes with their
heels, For I am proverb'd with a grandsire
phrase; I'll be a candle-holder, and look
on. The game was ne'er so fair, and I am
done.

MERCUTIO

Tut, dun's the mouse, the constable's own
word: If thou art dun, we'll draw thee from
the mire Of this sir-reverence love,
wherein thou stick'st Up to the ears. Come,
we burn daylight, ho!

ROMEO

Nay, that's not so.

MERCUTIO

I mean, sir, in delay We waste our lights
in vain, like lamps by day. Take our good
meaning, for our judgment sits Five times
in that ere once in our five wits.

ROMEO

And we mean well in going to this mask; But
'tis no wit to go.

MERCUTIO

Why, may one ask?

ROMEO

I dream'd a dream to-night.

MERCUTIO

And so did I.

ROMEO

Well, what was yours?

MERCUTIO

That dreamers often lie.

ROMEO

In bed asleep, while they do dream things true.

MERCUTIO

O, then, I see Queen Mab hath been with you. She is the fairies' midwife, and she comes In shape no bigger than an agate-stone On the fore-finger of an alderman, Drawn with a team of little atomies Athwart men's noses as they lie asleep; Her wagon-spokes made of long spiders' legs, The cover of the wings of grasshoppers, The traces of the smallest spider's web, The collars of the moonshine's watery beams, Her whip of cricket's bone, the lash of film, Her wagoner a small grey-coated gnat, Not so big as a round little worm Prick'd from the lazy finger of a maid; Her chariot is an empty hazel-nut Made by the joiner squirrel or old grub, Time out o' mind the fairies' coachmakers. And in this state she gallops night by night Through lovers' brains, and then they dream of love; O'er courtiers' knees, that dream on court'sies straight, O'er lawyers' fingers, who straight dream on fees, O'er ladies ' lips, who straight on kisses dream, Which oft the angry Mab with blisters plagues, Because their breaths with sweetmeats tainted are: Sometime she gallops o'er a courtier's nose, And then dreams he of smelling out a suit; And sometime comes she with a tithe-pig's tail Tickling a parson's nose as a' lies asleep, Then dreams, he of another benefice: Sometime she driveth o'er a soldier's neck, And then dreams he of cutting foreign throats, Of breaches, ambuscadoes, Spanish blades, Of healths five-fathom deep; and then anon Drums in his ear, at which he starts and wakes, And being thus frighted swears a prayer or two And sleeps again. This is that very Mab That plats the manes of horses in the night, And bakes the elflocks in foul sluttish hairs, Which once untangled, much misfortune bodes: This is the hag, when maids lie on their backs, That presses them and learns them first to bear, Making them women of good carriage: This is she--

ROMEO

Peace, peace, Mercutio, peace! Thou talk'st of nothing.

MERCUTIO

True, I talk of dreams, Which are the children of an idle brain, Begot of nothing but vain fantasy, Which is as thin of substance as the air And more inconstant than the wind, who wooes Even now the

frozen bosom of the north, And, being
anger'd, puffs away from thence, Turning his
face to the dew-dropping south.

BENVOLIO

This wind, you talk of, blows us from
ourselves; Supper is done, and we shall
come too late.

ROMEO

I fear, too early: for my mind misgives
Some consequence yet hanging in the stars
Shall bitterly begin his fearful date With
this night's revels and expire the term Of
a despised life closed in my breast By some
vile forfeit of untimely death. But He,
that hath the steerage of my course, Direct
my sail! On, lusty gentlemen.

BENVOLIO

Strike, drum.

Exeunt

SCENE 5. A HALL IN CAPULET'S HOUSE.

Musicians waiting. Enter SERVINGMEN with napkins

FIRST SERVANT
> Where's Potpan, that he helps not to take
> away? He shift a trencher? he scrape a
> trencher!

SECOND SERVANT
> When good manners shall lie all in one or
> two men's hands and they unwashed too, 'tis
> a foul thing.

William Shakespeare

FIRST SERVANT

Away with the joint-stools, remove the
court-cupboard, look to the plate. Good
thou, save me a piece of marchpane; and, as
thou lovest me, let the porter let in Susan
Grindstone and Nell. Antony, and Potpan!

SECOND SERVANT

Ay, boy, ready.

FIRST SERVANT

You are looked for and called for, asked
for and sought for, in the great chamber.

SECOND SERVANT

We cannot be here and there too. Cheerly,
boys; be brisk awhile, and the longer liver
take all.

*Enter CAPULET, with JULIET and others of his
house, meeting the Guests and Maskers*

CAPULET

Welcome, gentlemen! ladies that have their
toes Unplagued with corns will have a bout
with you. Ah ha, my mistresses! which of
you all Will now deny to dance? she that
makes dainty, She, I'll swear, hath corns;
am I come near ye now? Welcome, gentlemen!
I have seen the day That I have worn a
visor and could tell A whispering tale in a
fair lady's ear, Such as would please: 'tis
gone, 'tis gone, 'tis gone: You are
welcome, gentlemen! come, musicians, play.
A hall, a hall! give room! and foot it,
girls.

Music plays, and they dance

CAPULET

More light, you knaves; and turn the tables
up, And quench the fire, the room is grown
too hot. Ah, sirrah, this unlook'd-for
sport comes well. Nay, sit, nay, sit, good
cousin Capulet; For you and I are past our
dancing days: How long is't now since last
yourself and I Were in a mask?

SECOND CAPULET

By'r lady, thirty years.

CAPULET

What, man! 'tis not so much, 'tis not so
much: 'Tis since the nuptials of Lucentio,
Come pentecost as quickly as it will, Some
five and twenty years; and then we mask'd.

SECOND CAPULET

'Tis more, 'tis more, his son is elder,
sir; His son is thirty.

CAPULET

Will you tell me that? His son was but a
ward two years ago.

ROMEO

(To a Servingman)
What lady is that, which doth enrich the
hand Of yonder knight?

SERVANT

I know not, sir.

ROMEO

O, she doth teach the torches to burn
bright! It seems she hangs upon the cheek
of night Like a rich jewel in an Ethiope's

e

ar; Beauty too rich for use, for earth too dear! So shows a snowy dove trooping with crows, As yonder lady o'er her fellows shows. The measure done, I'll watch her place of stand, And, touching hers, make blessed my rude hand. Did my heart love till now? forswear it, sight! For I ne'er saw true beauty till this night.

TYBALT

This, by his voice, should be a Montague. Fetch me my rapier, boy. What dares the slave Come hither, cover'd with an antic face, To fleer and scorn at our solemnity? Now, by the stock and honour of my kin, To strike him dead, I hold it not a sin.

CAPULET

Why, how now, kinsman! wherefore storm you so?

TYBALT

Uncle, this is a Montague, our foe, A villain that is hither come in spite, To scorn at our solemnity this night.

CAPULET

Young Romeo is it?

TYBALT

'Tis he, that villain Romeo.

CAPULET

Content thee, gentle coz, let him alone; He bears him like a portly gentleman; And, to say truth, Verona brags of him To be a virtuous and well-govern'd youth: I would not for the wealth of all the town Here in

my house do him disparagement: Therefore be
patient, take no note of him: It is my
will, the which if thou respect, Show a
fair presence and put off these frowns, And
ill-beseeming semblance for a feast.

TYBALT

It fits, when such a villain is a guest:
I'll not endure him.

CAPULET

He shall be endured: What, goodman boy! I
say, he shall: go to; Am I the master here,
or you? go to. You'll not endure him! God
shall mend my soul! You'll make a mutiny
among my guests! You will set cock-a-hoop!
you'll be the man!

TYBALT

Why, uncle, 'tis a shame.

CAPULET

Go to, go to; You are a saucy boy: is't so,
indeed? This trick may chance to scathe
you, I know what: You must contrary me!
marry, 'tis time. Well said, my hearts! You
are a princox; go: Be quiet, or--More
light, more light! For shame! I'll make you
quiet. What, cheerly, my hearts!

TYBALT

Patience perforce with wilful choler
meeting Makes my flesh tremble in their
different greeting. I will withdraw: but
this intrusion shall Now seeming sweet
convert to bitter gall.

TYBALT Exits

ROMEO

> (To Juliet)
> If I profane with my unworthiest hand This
> holy shrine, the gentle fine is this: My
> lips, two blushing pilgrims, ready stand To
> smooth that rough touch with a tender kiss.

JULIET

> Good pilgrim, you do wrong your hand too
> much, Which mannerly devotion shows in
> this; For saints have hands that pilgrims'
> hands do touch, And palm to palm is holy
> palmers' kiss.

ROMEO

> Have not saints lips, and holy palmers too?

JULIET

> Ay, pilgrim, lips that they must use in
> prayer.

ROMEO

> O, then, dear saint, let lips do what hands
> do; They pray, grant thou, lest faith turn
> to despair.

JULIET

> Saints do not move, though grant for
> prayers' sake.

ROMEO

> Then move not, while my prayer's effect I
> take. Thus from my lips, by yours, my sin
> is purged.

JULIET

> Then have my lips the sin that they have
> took.

ROMEO

Sin from thy lips? O trespass sweetly
urged! Give me my sin again.

JULIET

You kiss by the book.

NURSE

Madam, your mother craves a word with you.

ROMEO

What is her mother?

NURSE

Marry, bachelor, Her mother is the lady of
the house, And a good lady, and a wise and
virtuous I nursed her daughter, that you
talk'd withal; I tell you, he that can lay
hold of her Shall have the chinks.

ROMEO

Is she a Capulet? O dear account! my life
is my foe's debt.

BENVOLIO

Away, begone; the sport is at the best.

ROMEO

Ay, so I fear; the more is my unrest.

CAPULET

Nay, gentlemen, prepare not to be gone; We
have a trifling foolish banquet towards. Is
it e'en so? why, then, I thank you all I
thank you, honest gentlemen; good night.
More torches here! Come on then, let's to
bed. Ah, sirrah, by my fay, it waxes late:
I'll to my rest.

William Shakespeare

Exeunt all but JULIET and NURSE

JULIET

Come hither, nurse. What is yond gentleman?

NURSE

The son and heir of old Tiberio.

JULIET

What's he that now is going out of door?

NURSE

Marry, that, I think, be young Petrucio.

JULIET

What's he that follows there, that would
not dance?

NURSE

I know not.

JULIET

Go ask his name: if he be married. My grave
is like to be my wedding bed.

NURSE

His name is Romeo, and a Montague; The only
son of your great enemy.

JULIET

My only love sprung from my only hate! Too
early seen unknown, and known too late!
Prodigious birth of love it is to me, That
I must love a loathed enemy.

NURSE

What's this? what's this?

JULIET

> A rhyme I learn'd even now Of one I danced
> withal. One calls within 'Juliet.'

NURSE

> Anon, anon! Come, let's away; the strangers
> all are gone.

Exeunt

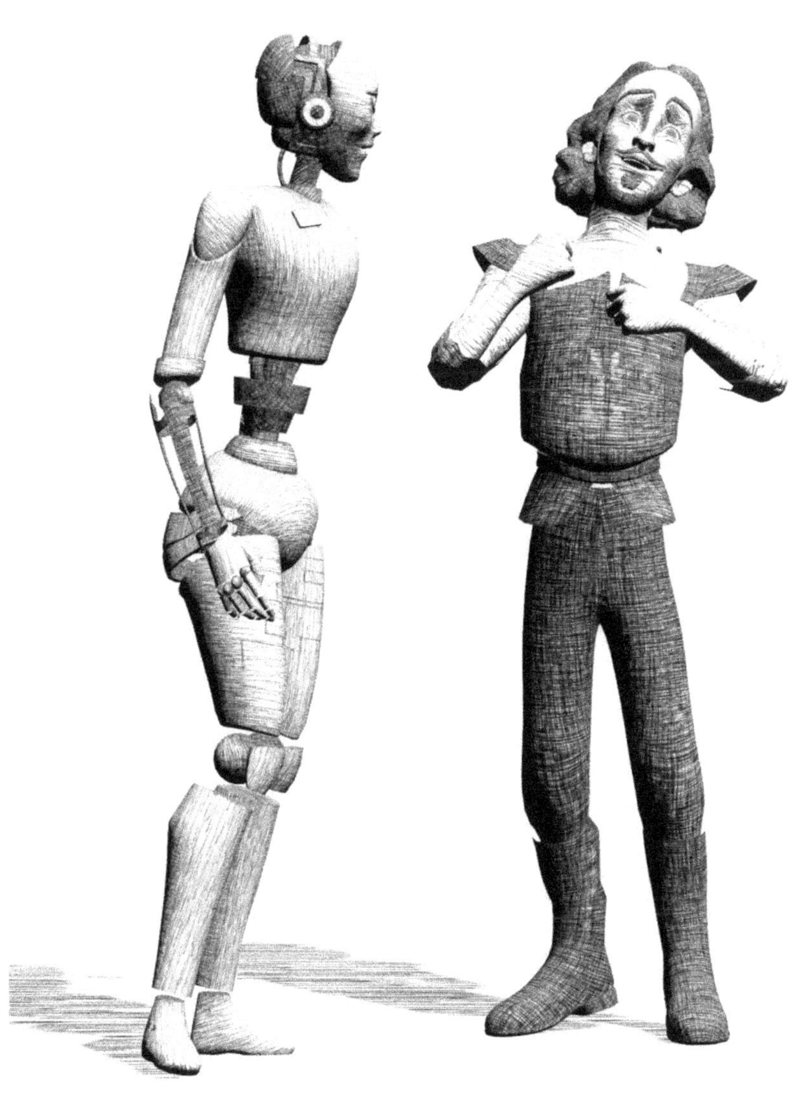

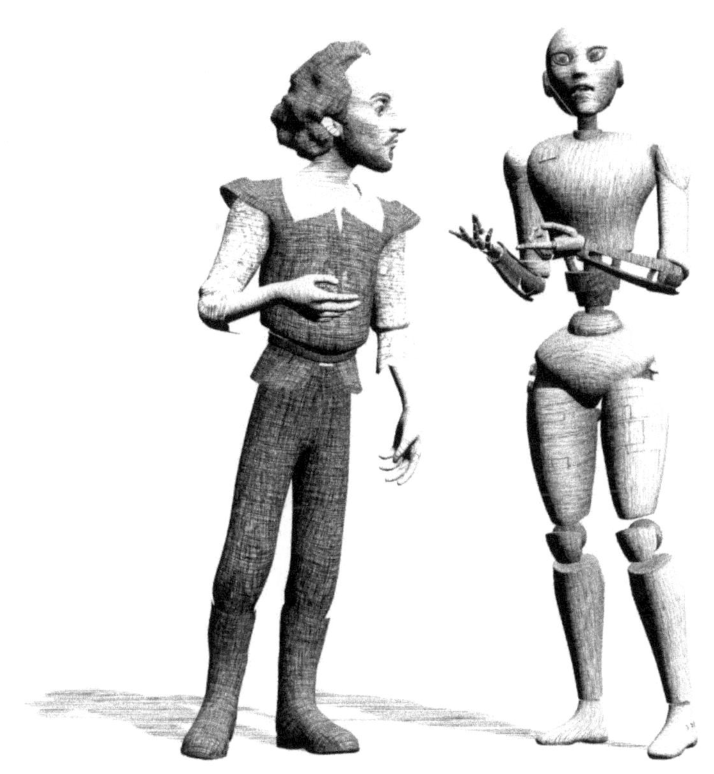

ACT II

PROLOGUE

Enter CHORUS

CHORUS

> Now old desire doth in his death-bed lie,
> And young affection gapes to be his heir;
> That fair for which love groan'd for and
> would die, With tender Juliet match'd, is
> now not fair. Now Romeo is beloved and
> loves again, Alike betwitched by the charm

of looks, But to his foe supposed he must
complain, And she steal love's sweet bait
from fearful hooks: Being held a foe, he
may not have access To breathe such vows as
lovers use to swear; And she as much in
love, her means much less To meet her new-
beloved any where: But passion lends them
power, time means, to meet Tempering
extremities with extreme sweet.

Exit

SCENE 1. A LANE BY THE WALL OF CAPULET'S ORCHARD.

Enter ROMEO

ROMEO

> Can I go forward when my heart is here?
> Turn back, dull earth, and find thy centre
> out. He climbs the wall, and leaps down
> within it

Enter BENVOLIO and MERCUTIO

BENVOLIO

> Romeo! my cousin Romeo!

MERCUTIO

>He is wise; And, on my lie, hath stol'n him
>home to bed.

BENVOLIO

>He ran this way, and leap'd this orchard
>wall: Call, good Mercutio.

MERCUTIO

>Nay, I'll conjure too. Romeo! humours!
>madman! passion! lover! Appear thou in the
>likeness of a sigh: Speak but one rhyme,
>and I am satisfied; Cry but 'Ay me!'
>pronounce but 'love' and 'dove;' Speak to
>my gossip Venus one fair word, One nick-
>name for her purblind son and heir, Young
>Adam Cupid, he that shot so trim, When King
>Cophetua loved the beggar-maid! He heareth
>not, he stirreth not, he moveth not; The
>ape is dead, and I must conjure him. I
>conjure thee by Rosaline's bright eyes, By
>her high forehead and her scarlet lip, By
>her fine foot, straight leg and quivering
>thigh And the demesnes that there adjacent
>lie, That in thy likeness thou appear to
>us!

BENVOLIO

>And if he hear thee, thou wilt anger him.

MERCUTIO

>This cannot anger him: 'twould anger him To
>raise a spirit in his mistress' circle Of
>some strange nature, letting it there stand
>Till she had laid it and conjured it down;
>That were some spite: my invocation Is fair
>and honest, and in his mistres s' name I
>conjure only but to raise up him.

BENVOLIO

> Come, he hath hid himself among these trees, To be consorted with the humorous night: Blind is his love and best befits the dark.

MERCUTIO

> If love be blind, love cannot hit the mark. Now will he sit under a medlar tree, And wish his mistress were that kind of fruit As maids call medlars, when they laugh alone. Romeo, that she were, O, that she were An open et caetera, thou a poperin pear! Romeo, good night: I'll to my truckle-bed; This field-bed is too cold for me to sleep: Come, shall we go?

BENVOLIO

> Go, then; for 'tis in vain To seek him here that means not to be found.

Exeunt

SCENE 2. CAPULET'S ORCHARD.

Enter ROMEO

ROMEO

> He jests at scars that never felt a wound.
> (JULIET appears above at a window)
> But, soft! what light through yonder window
> breaks? It is the east, and Juliet is the
> sun. Arise, fair sun, and kill the envious
> moon, Who is already sick and pale with
> grief, That thou her maid art far more fair
> than she: Be not her maid, since she is
> envious; Her vestal livery is but sick and

green And none but fools do wear it; cast it off. It is my lady, O, it is my love! O, that she knew she were! She speaks yet she says nothing: what of that? Her eye discourses; I will answer it. I am too bold, 'tis not to me she speaks: Two of the fairest stars in all the heaven, Having some business, do entreat her eyes To twinkle in their spheres till they return. What if her eyes were there, they in her head? The brightness of her cheek would shame those stars, As daylight doth a lamp; her eyes in heaven Would through the airy region stream so bright That birds would sing and think it were not night. See, how she leans her cheek upon her hand! O, that I were a glove upon that hand, That I might touch that cheek!

JULIET

Ay me!

ROMEO

She speaks: O, speak again, bright angel! for thou art As glorious to this night, being o'er my head As is a winged messenger of heaven Unto the white-upturned wondering eyes Of mortals that fall back to gaze on him When he bestrides the lazy-pacing clouds And sails upon the bosom of the air.

JULIET

O Romeo, Romeo! wherefore art thou Romeo? Deny thy father and refuse thy name; Or, if thou wilt not, be but sworn my love, And I'll no longer be a Capulet.

ROMEO

(Aside)
Shall I hear more, or shall I speak at
this?

JULIET

'Tis but thy name that is my enemy; Thou
art thyself, though not a Montague. What's
Montague? it is nor hand, nor foot, Nor
arm, nor face, nor any other part Belonging
to a man. O, be some other name! What's in
a name? that which we call a rose By any
other name would smell as sweet; So Romeo
would, were he not Romeo call'd, Retain
that dear perfection which he owes Without
that title. Romeo, doff thy name, And for
that name which is no part of thee Take all
myself.

ROMEO

I take thee at thy word: Call me but love,
and I'll be new baptized; Henceforth I
never will be Romeo.

JULIET

What man art thou that thus bescreen'd in
night So stumblest on my counsel?

ROMEO

By a name I know not how to tell thee who I
am: My name, dear saint, is hateful to
myself, Because it is an enemy to thee; Had
I it written, I would tear the word.

JULIET

My ears have not yet drunk a hundred words
Of that tongue's utterance, yet I know the
sound: Art thou not Romeo and a Montague?

ROMEO

Neither, fair saint, if either thee
dislike.

JULIET

How camest thou hither, tell me, and
wherefore? The orchard walls are high and
hard to climb, And the place death,
considering who thou art, If any of my
kinsmen find thee here.

ROMEO

With love's light wings did I o'er-perch
these walls;
For stony limits cannot hold love out, And
what love can do that dares love attempt;
Therefore thy kinsmen are no let to me.

JULIET

If they do see thee, they will murder thee.

ROMEO

Alack, there lies more peril in thine eye
Than twenty of their swords: look thou but
sweet, And I am proof against their enmity.

JULIET

I would not for the world they saw thee
here.

ROMEO

I have night's cloak to hide me from their
sight; And but thou love me, let them find
me here: My life were better ended by their
hate, Than death prorogued, wanting of thy
love.

JULIET

By whose direction found'st thou out this
place?

ROMEO

By love, who first did prompt me to inquire;
He lent me counsel and I lent him eyes. I
am no pilot; yet, wert thou as far As that
vast shore wash'd with the farthest sea, I
would adventure for such merchandise.

JULIET

Thou know'st the mask of night is on my
face, Else would a maiden blush bepaint my
cheek For that which thou hast heard me
speak to-night Fain would I dwell on form,
fain, fain deny What I have spoke: but
farewell compliment! Dost thou love me? I
know thou wilt say 'Ay,' And I will take
thy word: yet if thou swear'st, Thou mayst
prove false; at lovers' perjuries Then say,
Jove laughs. O gentle Romeo, If thou dost
love, pronounce it faithfully: Or if thou
think'st I am too quickly won, I'll frown
and be perverse an say thee nay, So thou
wilt woo; but else, not for the world. In
truth, fair Montague, I am too fond, And
therefore thou mayst think my 'havior
light: But trust me, gentleman, I'll prove
more true Than those that have more cunning
to be strange. I should have been more
strange, I must confess, But that thou
overheard'st, ere I was ware, My true
love's passion: therefore pardon me, And
not impute this yielding to light love,
Which the dark night hath so discovered.

ROMEO

Lady, by yonder blessed moon I swear That tips with silver all these fruit-tree tops-

JULIET

O, swear not by the moon, the inconstant moon, That monthly changes in her circled orb, Lest that thy love prove likewise variable.

ROMEO

What shall I swear by?

JULIET

Do not swear at all; Or, if thou wilt, swear by thy gracious self, Which is the god of my idolatry, And I'll believe thee.

ROMEO

If my heart's dear love--

JULIET

Well, do not swear: although I joy in thee, I have no joy of this contract to-night: It is too rash, too unadvised, too sudden; Too like the lightning, which doth cease to be Ere one can say 'It lightens.' Sweet, good night! This bud of love, by summer's ripening breath, May prove a beauteous flower when next we meet. Good night, good night! as sweet repose and rest Come to thy heart as that within my breast!

ROMEO

O, wilt thou leave me so unsatisfied?

JULIET

What satisfaction canst thou have to-night?

ROMEO

The exchange of thy love's faithful vow for mine.

JULIET

I gave thee mine before thou didst request it: And yet I would it were to give again.

ROMEO

Wouldst thou withdraw it? for what purpose, love?

JULIET

But to be frank, and give it thee again. And yet I wish but for the thing I have: My bounty is as boundless as the sea, My love as deep; the more I give to thee, The more I have, for both are infinite.
(Nurse calls within)
I hear some noise within; dear love, adieu! Anon, good nurse! Sweet Montague, be true. Stay but a little, I will come again.

Exit, above

ROMEO

O blessed, blessed night! I am afeard. Being in night, all this is but a dream, Too flattering-sweet to be substantial.

Re-enter JULIET, above

JULIET

Three words, dear Romeo, and good night indeed. If that thy bent of love be honourable, Thy purpose marriage, send me word to-morrow, By one that I'll procure to come to thee, Where and what time thou wilt

perform the rite; And all my fortunes at
thy foot I'll lay And follow thee my lord
throughout the world.

NURSE

(Within)
Madam!

JULIET

I come, anon.--But if thou mean'st not
well, I do beseech thee--

NURSE

(Within)
Madam!

JULIET

By and by, I come:— To cease thy suit, and
leave me to my grief: To-morrow will I
send.

ROMEO

So thrive my soul--

JULIET

A thousand times good night!

Exit, above

ROMEO

A thousand times the worse, to want thy
light. Love goes toward love, as schoolboys
from their books, But love from love,
toward school with heavy looks.
(Retiring)

Re-enter JULIET, above

JULIET

> Hist! Romeo, hist! O, for a falconer's voice, To lure this tassel-gentle back again! Bondage is hoarse, and may not speak aloud; Else would I tear the cave where Echo lies, And make her airy tongue more hoarse than mine, With repetition of my Romeo's name.

ROMEO

> It is my soul that calls upon my name: How silver-sweet sound lovers' tongues by night, Like softest music to attending ears!

JULIET

> Romeo!

ROMEO

> My dear?

JULIET

> At what o'clock to-morrow Shall I send to thee?

ROMEO

> At the hour of nine.

JULIET

> I will not fail: 'tis twenty years till then. I have forgot why I did call thee back.

ROMEO

> Let me stand here till thou remember it.

JULIET

> I shall forget, to have thee still stand
> there, Remembering how I love thy company.

ROMEO

> And I'll still stay, to have thee still
> forget, Forgetting any other home but this.

JULIET

> 'Tis almost morning; I would have thee
> gone: And yet no further than a wanton's
> bird; Who lets it hop a little from her
> hand, Like a poor prisoner in his twisted
> gyves, And with a silk thread plucks it
> back again, So loving-jealous of his
> liberty.

ROMEO

> I would I were thy bird.

JULIET

> Sweet, so would I: Yet I should kill thee
> with much cherishing. Good night, good
> night! parting is such sweet sorrow, That I
> shall say good night till it be morrow.

Exit above

ROMEO

> Sleep dwell upon thine eyes, peace in thy
> breast! Would I were sleep and peace, so
> sweet to rest! Hence will I to my ghostly
> father's cell, His help to crave, and my
> dear hap to tell.

Exit

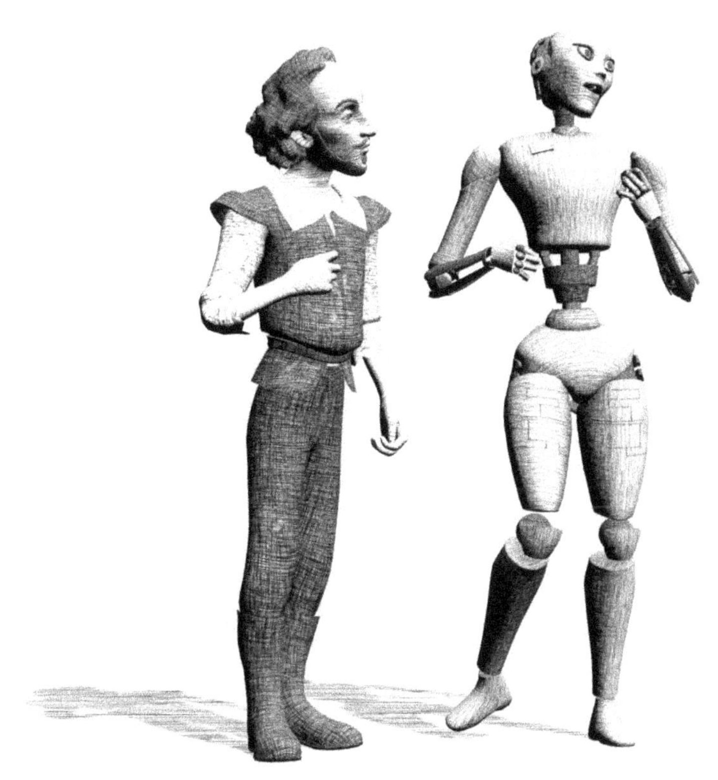

SCENE 3. FRIAR LAURENCE'S CELL.

Enter FRIAR LAURENCE, with a basket

FRIAR LAURENCE
The grey-eyed morn smiles on the frowning
night, Chequering the eastern clouds with
streaks of light, And flecked darkness like
a drunkard reels From forth day's path and
Titan's fiery wheels: Now, ere the sun
advance his burning eye, The day to cheer
and night's dank dew to dry, I must up-fill
this osier cage of ours With baleful weeds
and precious-juiced flowers. The earth

that's nature's mother is her tomb; What is
her burying grave that is her womb, And
from her womb children of divers kind We
sucking on her natural bosom find, Many for
many virtues excellent, None but for some
and yet all different. O, mickle is the
powerful grace that lies In herbs, plants,
stones, and their true qualities: For
nought so vile that on the earth doth live
But to the earth some special good doth
give, Nor aught so good but strain'd from
that fair use Revolts from true birth,
stumbling on abuse: Virtue itself turns
vice, being misapplied; And vice sometimes
by action dignified. Within the infant rind
of this small flower Poison hath residence
and medicine power: For this, being smelt,
with that part cheers each part; Being
tasted, slays all senses with the heart.
Two such opposed kings encamp them still In
man as well as herbs, grace and rude will;
And where the worser is predominant, Full
soon the canker death eats up that plant.

Enter ROMEO

ROMEO

Good morrow, father.

FRIAR LAURENCE

Benedicite! What early tongue so sweet
saluteth me? Young son, it argues a
distemper'd head So soon to bid good morrow
to thy bed: Care keeps his watch in every
old man's eye, And where care lodges, sleep
will never lie; But where unbruised youth
with unstuff'd brain Doth couch his limbs,
there golden sleep doth reign: Therefore

thy earliness doth me assure Thou art up-
roused by some distemperature; Or if not
so, then here I hit it right, Our Romeo
hath not been in bed to-night.

ROMEO

That last is true; the sweeter rest was
mine.

FRIAR LAURENCE

God pardon sin! wast thou with Rosaline?

ROMEO

With Rosaline, my ghostly father? no; I
have forgot that name, and that name's woe.

FRIAR LAURENCE

That's my good son: but where hast thou
been, then?

ROMEO

I'll tell thee, ere thou ask it me again. I
have been feasting with mine enemy, Where
on a sudden one hath wounded me, That's by
me wounded: both our remedies Within thy
help and holy physic lies: I bear no
hatred, blessed man, for, lo, My
intercession likewise steads my foe.

FRIAR LAURENCE

Be plain, good son, and homely in thy
drift;
Riddling confession finds but riddling
shrift.

ROMEO

Then plainly know my heart's dear love is
set

On the fair daughter of rich Capulet:
As mine on hers, so hers is set on mine;
And all combined, save what thou must
combine
By holy marriage: when and where and how
We met, we woo'd and made exchange of vow,
I'll tell thee as we pass; but this I pray,
That thou consent to marry us to-day.

FRIAR LAURENCE

Holy Saint Francis, what a change is here!
Is Rosaline, whom thou didst love so dear,
So soon forsaken? young men's love then
lies
Not truly in their hearts, but in their
eyes.
Jesu Maria, what a deal of brine
Hath wash'd thy sallow cheeks for Rosaline!
How much salt water thrown away in waste,
To season love, that of it doth not taste!
The sun not yet thy sighs from heaven
clears,
Thy old groans ring yet in my ancient ears;
Lo, here upon thy cheek the stain doth sit
Of an old tear that is not wash'd off yet:
If e'er thou wast thyself and these woes
thine,
Thou and these woes were all for Rosaline:
And art thou changed? pronounce this
sentence then,
Women may fall, when there's no strength in
men.

ROMEO

Thou chid'st me oft for loving Rosaline.

FRIAR LAURENCE

For doting, not for loving, pupil mine.

ROMEO

> And bad'st me bury love.

FRIAR LAURENCE

> Not in a grave, To lay one in, another out
> to have.

ROMEO

> I pray thee, chide not; she whom I love now
> Doth grace for grace and love for love
> allow; The other did not so.

FRIAR LAURENCE

> O, she knew well Thy love did read by rote
> and could not spell. But come, young
> waverer, come, go with me, In one respect
> I'll thy assistant be; For this alliance
> may so happy prove, To turn your
> households' rancour to pure love.

ROMEO

> O, let us hence; I stand on sudden haste.

FRIAR LAURENCE

> Wisely and slow; they stumble that run
> fast.

Exeunt

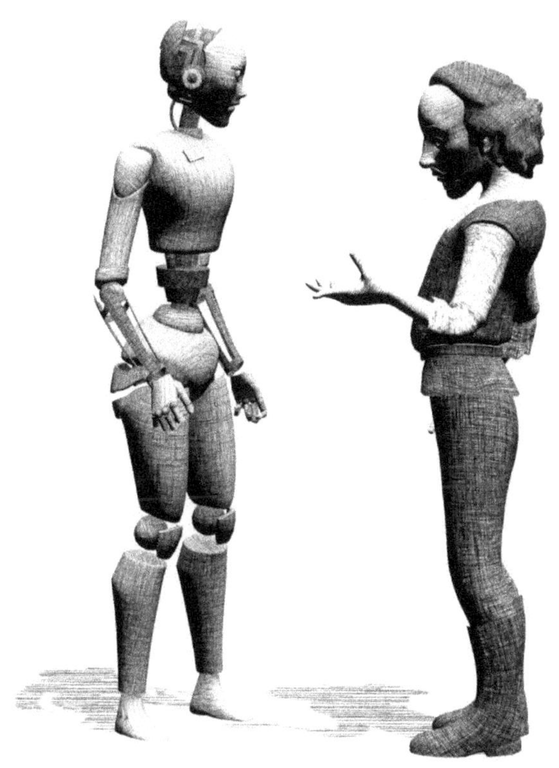

SCENE 4. A STREET.

Enter BENVOLIO and MERCUTIO

MERCUTIO

    Where the devil should this Romeo be? Came
    he not home to-night?

BENVOLIO

    Not to his father's; I spoke with his man.

MERCUTIO

    Ah, that same pale hard-hearted wench, that

Rosaline. Torments him so, that he will
sure run mad.

BENVOLIO

Tybalt, the kinsman of old Capulet, Hath
sent a letter to his father's house.

MERCUTIO

A challenge, on my life.

BENVOLIO

Romeo will answer it.

MERCUTIO

Any man that can write may answer a letter.

BENVOLIO

Nay, he will answer the letter's master,
how he dares, being dared.

MERCUTIO

Alas poor Romeo! he is already dead;
stabbed with a white wench's black eye;
shot through the ear with a love-song; the
very pin of his heart cleft with the blind
bow-boy's butt-shaft: and is he a man to
encounter Tybalt?

BENVOLIO

Why, what is Tybalt?

MERCUTIO

More than prince of cats, I can tell you.
O, he is the courageous captain of
compliments. He fights as you sing prick-
song, keeps time, distance, and proportion;
rests me his minim rest, one, two, and the
third in your bosom: the very butcher of a

silk button, a duellist, a duellist; a
gentleman of the very first house, of the
first and second cause: ah, the immortal
passado! the punto reverso! the hai!

BENVOLIO

The what?

MERCUTIO

The pox of such antic, lisping, affecting
fantasticoes; these new tuners of accents!
'By Jesu, a very good blade! a very tall
man! a very good whore!' Why, is not this a
lamentable thing, grandsire, that we should
be thus afflicted with these strange flies,
these fashion-mongers, these perdona-mi's,
who stand so much on the new form, that
they cannot at ease on the old bench? O,
their bones, their bones!

Enter ROMEO

BENVOLIO

Here comes Romeo, here comes Romeo.

MERCUTIO

Without his roe, like a dried herring:
flesh, flesh, how art thou fishified! Now is he
for the numbers that Petrarch flowed in:
Laura to his lady was but a kitchen-wench;
marry, she had a better love to be-rhyme
her; Dido a dowdy; Cleopatra a gipsy; Helen
and Hero hildings and harlots; Thisbe a
grey eye or so, but not to the purpose.
Signior Romeo, bon jour! there's a French
salutation to your French slop. You gave us
the counterfeit fairly last night.

ROMEO

Good morrow to you both. What counterfeit
did I give you?

MERCUTIO

The ship, sir, the slip; can you not
conceive?

ROMEO

Pardon, good Mercutio, my business was
great; and in such a case as mine a man may
strain courtesy.

MERCUTIO

That's as much as to say, such a case as
yours constrains a man to bow in the hams.

ROMEO

Meaning, to court'sy.

MERCUTIO

Thou hast most kindly hit it.

ROMEO

A most courteous exposition.

MERCUTIO

Nay, I am the very pink of courtesy.

ROMEO

Pink for flower.

MERCUTIO

Right.

ROMEO

Why, then is my pump well flowered.

MERCUTIO

> Well said: follow me this jest now till
> thou hast worn out thy pump, that when the
> single sole of it is worn, the jest may
> remain after the wearing sole singular.

ROMEO

> O single-soled jest, solely singular for
> the singleness.

MERCUTIO

> Come between us, good Benvolio; my wits
> faint.

ROMEO

> Switch and spurs, switch and spurs; or I'll
> cry a match.

MERCUTIO

> Nay, if thy wits run the wild-goose chase,
> I have done, for thou hast more of the
> wild-goose in one of thy wits than, I am
> sure, I have in my whole five: was I with
> you there for the goose?

ROMEO

> Thou wast never with me for any thing when
> thou wast not there for the goose.

MERCUTIO

> I will bite thee by the ear for that jest.

ROMEO

> Nay, good goose, bite not.

MERCUTIO

> Thy wit is a very bitter sweeting; it is a
> most sharp sauce.

ROMEO

And is it not well served in to a sweet
goose?

MERCUTIO

O here's a wit of cheveril, that stretches
from an inch narrow to an ell broad!

ROMEO

I stretch it out for that word 'broad;'
which added to the goose, proves thee far
and wide a broad goose.

MERCUTIO

Why, is not this better now than groaning
for love? now art thou sociable, now art
thou Romeo; now art thou what thou art, by
art as well as by nature: for this
drivelling love is like a great natural,
that runs lolling up and down to hide his
bauble in a hole.

BENVOLIO

Stop there, stop there.

MERCUTIO

Thou desirest me to stop in my tale against
the hair.

BENVOLIO

Thou wouldst else have made thy tale large.

MERCUTIO

O, thou art deceived; I would have made it
short: for I was come to the whole depth of
my tale; and meant, indeed, to occupy the
argument no longer.

ROMEO

Here's goodly gear!

Enter Nurse and PETER

MERCUTIO

A sail, a sail!

BENVOLIO

Two, two; a shirt and a smock.

NURSE

Peter!

PETER

Anon!

NURSE

My fan, Peter.

MERCUTIO

Good Peter, to hide her face; for her fan's the fairer face.

NURSE

God ye good morrow, gentlemen.

MERCUTIO

God ye good den, fair gentlewoman.

NURSE

Is it good den?

MERCUTIO

'Tis no less, I tell you, for the bawdy hand of the dial is now upon the prick of noon.

NURSE

Out upon you! what a man are you!

ROMEO

One, gentlewoman, that God hath made for himself to mar.

NURSE

By my troth, it is well said; 'for himself to mar,' quoth a'? Gentlemen, can any of you tell me where I may find the young Romeo?

ROMEO

I can tell you; but young Romeo will be older when you have found him than he was when you sought him: I am the youngest of that name, for fault of a worse.

NURSE

You say well.

MERCUTIO

Yea, is the worst well? very well took, i' faith; wisely, wisely.

NURSE

if you be he, sir, I desire some confidence with you.

BENVOLIO

She will indite him to some supper.

MERCUTIO

A bawd, a bawd, a bawd! so ho!

ROMEO

What hast thou found?

MERCUTIO

> No hare, sir; unless a hare, sir, in a
> lenten pie, that is something stale and
> hoar ere it be spent.
> (Sings)
> An old hare hoar, And an old hare hoar, Is
> very good meat in lent But a hare that is
> hoar Is too much for a score, When it hoars
> ere it be spent. Romeo, will you come to
> your father's? we'll to dinner, thither.

ROMEO

> I will follow you.

MERCUTIO

> Farewell, ancient lady; farewell,
> (Singing)
> 'lady, lady, lady.'

Exeunt MERCUTIO and BENVOLIO

NURSE

> Marry, farewell! I pray you, sir, what
> saucy merchant was this, that was so full
> of his ropery?

ROMEO

> A gentleman, nurse, that loves to hear
> himself talk, and will speak more in a
> minute than he will stand to in a month.

NURSE

> An a' speak any thing against me, I'll take
> him down, an a' were lustier than he is,
> and twenty such Jacks; and if I cannot,
> I'll find those that shall. Scurvy knave! I
> am none of his flirt-gills; I am none of his
> skains-mates. And thou must stand by too,

and suffer every knave to use me at his
pleasure?

PETER

I saw no man use you a pleasure; if I had,
my weapon should quickly have been out, I
warrant you: I dare draw as soon as another
man, if I see occasion in a good quarrel,
and the law on my side.

NURSE

Now, afore God, I am so vexed, that every
part about me quivers. Scurvy knave! Pray
you, sir, a word: and as I told you, my
young lady bade me inquire you out; what
she bade me say, I will keep to myself: but
first let me tell ye, if ye should lead her
into a fool's paradise, as they say, it
were a very gross kind of behavior, as they
say: for the gentlewoman is young; and,
therefore, if you should deal double with
her, truly it were an ill thing to be
offered to any gentlewoman, and very weak
dealing.

ROMEO

Nurse, commend me to thy lady and mistress.
I protest unto thee--

NURSE

Good heart, and, i' faith, I will tell her
as much: Lord, Lord, she will be a joyful
woman.

ROMEO

What wilt thou tell her, nurse? thou dost
not mark me.

NURSE

> I will tell her, sir, that you do protest;
> which, as I take it, is a gentlemanlike
> offer.

ROMEO

> Bid her devise Some means to come to shrift
> this afternoon; And there she shall at
> Friar Laurence' cell Be shrived and
> married. Here is for thy pains.

NURSE

> No truly sir; not a penny.

ROMEO

> Go to; I say you shall.

NURSE

> This afternoon, sir? well, she shall be
> there.

ROMEO

> And stay, good nurse, behind the abbey
> wall: Within this hour my man shall be with
> thee And bring thee cords made like a
> tackled stair; Which to the high top-
> gallant of my joy Must be my convoy in the
> secret night. Farewell; be trusty, and I'll
> quit thy pains: Farewell; commend me to thy
> mistress.

NURSE

> Now God in heaven bless thee! Hark you,
> sir.

ROMEO

> What say'st thou, my dear nurse?

NURSE

Is your man secret? Did you ne'er hear say,
Two may keep counsel, putting one away?

ROMEO

I warrant thee, my man's as true as steel.

NURSE

Well, sir; my mistress is the sweetest
lady—Lord, Lord! when 'twas a little
prating thing:--O, there is a nobleman in
town, one Paris, that would fain lay knife
aboard; but she, good soul, had as lief see
a toad, a very toad, as see him. I anger
her sometimes and tell her that Paris is
the properer man; but, I'll warrant you,
when I say so, she looks as pale as any
clout in the versal world. Doth not
rosemary and Romeo begin both with a
letter?

ROMEO

Ay, nurse; what of that? both with an R.

NURSE

Ah. mocker! that's the dog's name; R is for
the--No; I know it begins with some other
letter:--and she hath the prettiest
sententious of it, of you and rosemary,
that it would do you good to hear it.

ROMEO

Commend me to thy lady.

NURSE

Ay, a thousand times. Peter!

Exit ROMEO

PETER

Anon!

NURSE

Peter, take my fan, and go before and
apace.

Exeunt

PETER

Anon!

NURSE

Peter, take my fan, and go before and
apace.

Exeunt

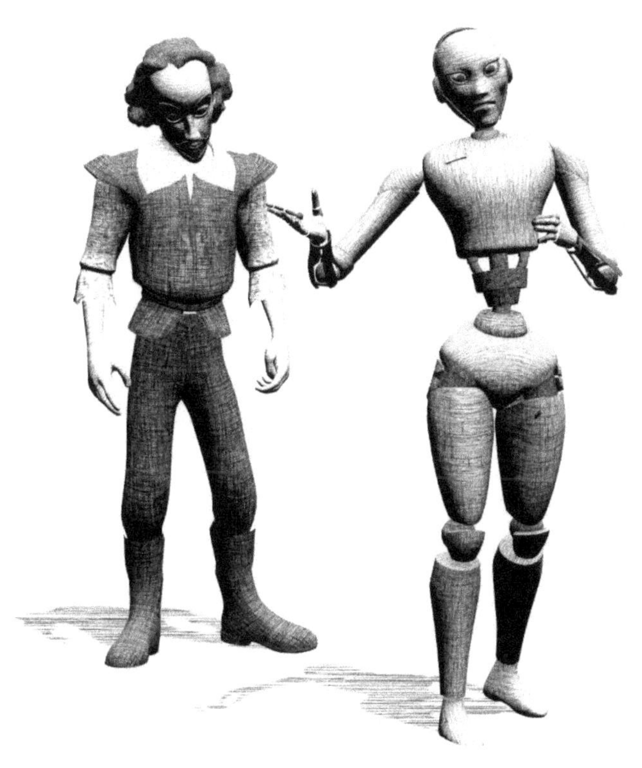

SCENE 5. CAPULET'S ORCHARD.

Enter JULIET

JULIET

>   The clock struck nine when I did send the
>   nurse; In half an hour she promised to
>   return. Perchance she cannot meet him:
>   that's not so. O, she is lame! love's
>   heralds should be thoughts, Which ten times
>   faster glide than the sun's beams, Driving
>   back shadows over louring hills: Therefore
>   do nimble-pinion'd doves draw love, And
>   therefore hath the wind-swift Cupid wings.

Now is the sun upon the highmost hill Of
this day's journey, and from nine till
twelve Is three long hours, yet she is not
come. Had she affections and warm youthful
blood, She would be as swift in motion as a
ball; My words would bandy her to my sweet
love, And his to me: But old folks, many
feign as they were dead; Unwieldy, slow,
heavy and pale as lead. O God, she comes!

Enter NURSE and PETER

JULIET

O honey nurse, what news?
Hast thou met with him? Send thy man away.

NURSE

Peter, stay at the gate.

Exit PETER

JULIET

Now, good sweet nurse,--O Lord, why look'st
thou sad? Though news be sad, yet tell them
merrily; If good, thou shamest the music of
sweet news By playing it to me with so sour
a face.

NURSE

I am a-weary, give me leave awhile: Fie,
how my bones ache! what a jaunt have I had!

JULIET

I would thou hadst my bones, and I thy
news: Nay, come, I pray thee, speak; good,
good nurse, speak.

NURSE

> Jesu, what haste? can you not stay awhile?
> Do you not see that I am out of breath?

JULIET

> How art thou out of breath, when thou hast
> breath To say to me that thou art out of
> breath? The excuse that thou dost make in
> this delay Is longer than the tale thou
> dost excuse. Is thy news good, or bad?
> answer to that; Say , and I'll stay the
> circumstance: Let me be satisfied, is't good
> or bad?

NURSE

> Well, you have made a simple choice; you
> know not how to choose a man: Romeo! no,
> not he; though his face be better than any
> man's, yet his leg excels all men's; and
> for a hand, and a foot, and a body, though
> they be not to be talked on, yet they are
> past compare: he is not the flower of
> courtesy, but, I'll warrant him, as gentle
> as a lamb. Go thy ways, wench; serve God.
> What, have you dined at home?

JULIET

> No, no: but all this did I know before.
> What says he of our marriage? what of that?

NURSE

> Lord, how my head aches! what a head have
> I! It beats as it would fall in twenty
> pieces. My back o' t' other side,--O, my
> back, my back! Beshrew your heart for
> sending me about, To catch my death with
> jaunting up and down!

JULIET

I' faith, I am sorry that thou art not
well. Sweet, sweet, sweet nurse, tell me,
what says my love?

NURSE

Your love says, like an honest gentleman,
and a courteous, and a kind, and a
handsome, and, I warrant, a virtuous,--
Where is your mother?

JULIET

Where is my mother! why, she is within;
Where should she be? How oddly thou
repliest! 'Your love says, like an honest
gentleman, Where is your mother?'

NURSE

O God's lady dear! Are you so hot? marry,
come up, I trow; Is this the poultice for
my aching bones? Henceforward do your
messages yourself.

JULIET

Here's such a coil! come, what says Romeo?

NURSE

Have you got leave to go to shrift to-day?

JULIET

I have.

NURSE

Then hie you hence to Friar Laurence' cell;
There stays a husband to make you a wife:
Now comes the wanton blood up in your
cheeks, They'll be in scarlet straight at
any news. Hie you to church; I must another

way, To fetch a ladder, by the which your
love Must climb a bird's nest soon when it
is dark: I am the drudge and toil in your
delight, But you shall bear the burden soon
at night. Go; I'll to dinner: hie you to
the cell.

JULIET

Hie to high fortune! Honest nurse,
farewell.

Exeunt

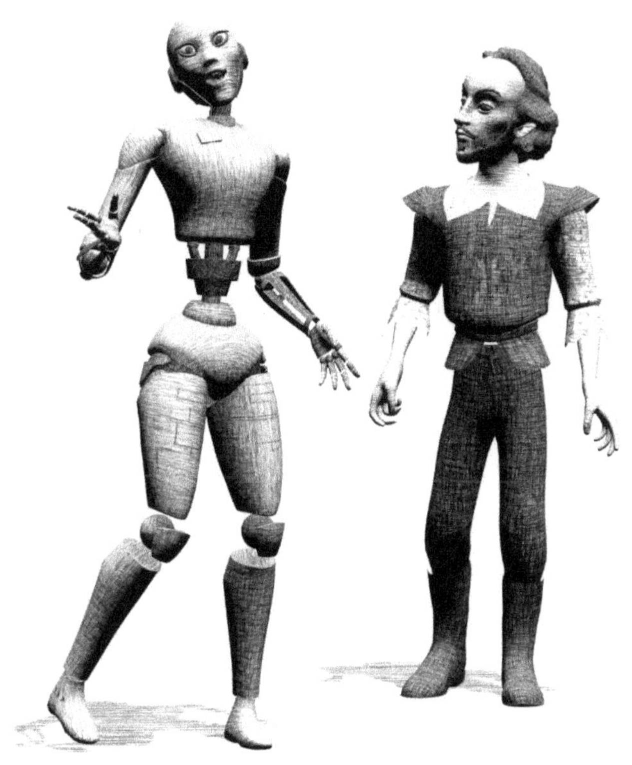

SCENE 6. FRIAR LAURENCE'S CELL.

Enter FRIAR LAURENCE and ROMEO

FRIAR LAURENCE
> So smile the heavens upon this holy act,
> That after hours with sorrow chide us not!

ROMEO
> Amen, amen! but come what sorrow can, It
> cannot countervail the exchange of joy That
> one short minute gives me in her sight: Do
> thou but close our hands with holy words,

Then love-devouring death do what he dare;
It is enough I may but call her mine.

FRIAR LAURENCE

These violent delights have violent ends
And in their triumph die, like fire and
powder, Which as they kiss consume: the
sweetest honey Is loathsome in his own
deliciousness And in the taste confounds
the appetite: Therefore love moderately;
long love doth so; Too swift arrives as
tardy as too slow.

Enter JULIET

FRIAR LAURENCE

Here comes the lady: O, so light a foot
Will ne'er wear out the everlasting flint: A
lover may bestride the gossamer That idles
in the wanton summer air, And yet not fall;
so light is vanity.

JULIET

Good even to my ghostly confessor.

FRIAR LAURENCE

Romeo shall thank thee, daughter, for us
both.

JULIET

As much to him, else is his thanks too
much.

ROMEO

Ah, Juliet, if the measure of thy joy Be
heap'd like mine and that thy skill be more
To blazon it, then sweeten with thy breath
This neighbour air, and let rich music's

tongue Unfold the imagined happiness that
both Receive in either by this dear
encounter.

JULIET

Conceit, more rich in matter than in words,
Brags of his substance, not of ornament:
They are but beggars that can count their
worth; But my true love is grown to such
excess I cannot sum up sum of half my
wealth.

FRIAR LAURENCE

Come, come with me, and we will make short
work; For, by your leaves, you shall not
stay alone Till holy church incorporate two
in one.

Exeunt

ACT III

SCENE 1. A PUBLIC PLACE.

Enter MERCUTIO, BENVOLIO, Page, and Servants

BENVOLIO
> I pray thee, good Mercutio, let's retire:
> The day is hot, the Capulets abroad, And,
> if we meet, we shall not scape a brawl; For
> now, these hot days, is the mad blood
> stirring.

MERCUTIO

Thou art like one of those fellows that
when he enters the confines of a tavern
claps me his sword upon the table and says
'God send me no need of thee!' and by the
operation of the second cup draws it on the
drawer, when indeed there is no need.

BENVOLIO

Am I like such a fellow?

MERCUTIO

Come, come, thou art as hot a Jack in thy
mood as any in Italy, and as soon moved to
be moody, and as soon moody to be moved.

BENVOLIO

And what to?

MERCUTIO

Nay, an there were two such, we should have
none shortly, for one would kill the other.
Thou! why, thou wilt quarrel with a man
that hath a hair more, or a hair less, in
his beard, than thou hast: thou wilt
quarrel with a man for cracking nuts,
having no other reason but because thou
hast hazel eyes: what eye but such an eye
would spy out such a quarrel? Thy head is
as fun of quarrels as an egg is full of
meat, and yet thy head hath been beaten as
addle as an egg for quarrelling: thou hast
quarrelled with a man for coughing the
street, because he hath wakened thy dog
that hath lain asleep in the sun: didst
thou not fall out with a tailor for wearing
his new doublet before Easter? with
another, for tying his new shoes with old

riband? and yet thou wilt tutor me from
quarrelling!

BENVOLIO

An I were so apt to quarrel as thou art,
any man should buy the fee-simple of my
life for an hour and a quarter.

MERCUTIO

The fee-simple! O simple!

BENVOLIO

By my head, here come the Capulets.

MERCUTIO

By my heel, I care not.

Enter TYBALT and others

TYBALT

Follow me close, for I will speak to them.
Gentlemen, good den: a word with one of
you.

MERCUTIO

And but one word with one of us? couple it
with something; make it a word and a blow.

TYBALT

You shall find me apt enough to that, sir,
an you will give me occasion.

MERCUTIO

Could you not take some occasion without
giving?

TYBALT

Mercutio, thou consort'st with Romeo,--

MERCUTIO

> Consort! what, dost thou make us minstrels?
> an thou make minstrels of us, look to hear
> nothing but discords: here's my fiddlestick;
> here's that shall make you dance. 'Zounds,
> consort!

BENVOLIO

> We talk here in the public haunt of men:
> Either withdraw unto some private place,
> And reason coldly of your grievances, Or
> else depart; here all eyes gaze on us.

MERCUTIO

> Men's eyes were made to look, and let them
> gaze; I will not budge for no man's
> pleasure, I.

Enter ROMEO

TYBALT

> Well, peace be with you, sir: here comes my
> man.

MERCUTIO

> But I'll be hanged, sir, if he wear your
> livery: Marry, go before to field, he'll be
> your follower; Your worship in that sense
> may call him 'man.'

TYBALT

> Romeo, the hate I bear thee can afford No
> better term than this,--thou art a villain.

ROMEO

> Tybalt, the reason that I have to love thee
> Doth much excuse the appertaining rage To
> such a greeting: villain am I none;

Therefore farewell; I see thou know'st me
not.

TYBALT

Boy, this shall not excuse the injuries
That thou hast done me; therefore turn and
draw.

ROMEO

I do protest, I never injured thee, But
love thee better than thou canst devise,
Till thou shalt know the reason of my love:
And so, good Capulet,--which name I tender
As dearly as my own,--be satisfied.

MERCUTIO

O calm, dishonourable, vile submission!
Alla stoccata carries it away.

Draws

MERCUTIO

Tybalt, you rat-catcher, will you walk?

TYBALT

What wouldst thou have with me?

MERCUTIO

Good king of cats, nothing but one of your
nine lives; that I mean to make bold
withal, and as you shall use me hereafter,
drybeat the rest of the eight. Will you
pluck your sword out of his pitcher by the
ears? make haste, lest mine be about your
ears ere it be out.

TYBALT

I am for you.

Drawing

ROMEO

Gentle Mercutio, put thy rapier up.

MERCUTIO

Come, sir, your passado.

They fight

ROMEO

Draw, Benvolio; beat down their weapons.
Gentlemen, for shame, forbear this outrage!
Tybalt, Mercutio, the prince expressly hath
Forbidden bandying in Verona streets: Hold,
Tybalt! good Mercutio!

*TYBALT under ROMEO's arm stabs MERCUTIO, and flies
with his followers*

MERCUTIO

I am hurt. A plague o' both your houses! I
am sped. Is he gone, and hath nothing?

BENVOLIO

What, art thou hurt?

MERCUTIO

Ay, ay, a scratch, a scratch; marry, 'tis
enough. Where is my page? Go, villain,
fetch a surgeon.

Exit Page

ROMEO

Courage, man; the hurt cannot be much.

MERCUTIO

> No, 'tis not so deep as a well, nor so wide
> as a church-door; but 'tis enough,'twill
> serve: ask for me to-morrow, and you shall
> find me a grave man. I am peppered, I
> warrant, for this world. A plague o' both
> your houses! 'Zounds, a dog, a rat, a
> mouse, a cat, to scratch a man to death! a
> braggart, a rogue, a villain, that fights by
> the book of arithmetic! Why the devil came
> you between us? I was hurt under your arm.

ROMEO

> I thought all for the best.

MERCUTIO

> Help me into some house, Benvolio, Or I
> shall faint. A plague o' both your houses!
> They have made worms' meat of me: I have
> it, And soundly too: your houses!

Exeunt MERCUTIO and BENVOLIO

ROMEO

> This gentleman, the prince's near ally, My
> very friend, hath got his mortal hurt In my
> behalf; my reputation stain'd With Tybalt's
> slander,--Tybalt, that an hour Hath been my
> kinsman! O sweet Juliet, Thy beauty hath
> made me effeminate And in my temper soften'd
> valour's steel!

Re-enter BENVOLIO

BENVOLIO

> O Romeo, Romeo, brave Mercutio's dead! That
> gallant spirit hath aspired the clouds,

Which too untimely here did scorn the
earth.

ROMEO

This day's black fate on more days doth
depend; This but begins the woe, others
must end.

BENVOLIO

Here comes the furious Tybalt back again.

ROMEO

Alive, in triumph! and Mercutio slain! Away
to heaven, respective lenity, And fire-eyed
fury be my conduct now!

Re-enter TYBALT

ROMEO

Now, Tybalt, take the villain back again,
That late thou gavest me; for Mercutio's
soul Is but a little way above our heads,
Staying for thine to keep him company:
Either thou, or I, or both, must go with
him.

TYBALT

Thou, wretched boy, that didst consort him
here, Shalt with him hence.

ROMEO

This shall determine that. They fight;
TYBALT falls

BENVOLIO

Romeo, away, be gone! The citizens are up,
and Tybalt slain. Stand not amazed: the

prince will doom thee death, If thou art
taken: hence, be gone, away!

ROMEO

O, I am fortune's fool!

BENVOLIO

Why dost thou stay?

Exit ROMEO

Enter Citizens

FIRST CITIZEN

Which way ran he that kill'd Mercutio?
Tybalt, that murderer, which way ran he?

BENVOLIO

There lies that Tybalt.

FIRST CITIZEN

Up, sir, go with me; I charge thee in the
princes name, obey.

*Enter PRINCE, attended; MONTAGUE, CAPULET, their
Wives, and others*

PRINCE

Where are the vile beginners of this fray?

BENVOLIO

O noble prince, I can discover all The
unlucky manage of this fatal brawl: There
lies the man, slain by young Romeo, That
slew thy kinsman, brave Mercutio.

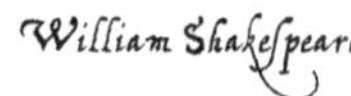

LADY CAPULET

Tybalt, my cousin! O my brother's child! O
prince! O cousin! husband! O, the blood is
spilt O my dear kinsman! Prince, as thou
art true, For blood of ours, shed blood of
Montague. O cousin, cousin!

PRINCE

Benvolio, who began this bloody fray?

BENVOLIO

Tybalt, here slain, whom Romeo's hand did
slay; Romeo that spoke him fair, bade him
bethink How nice the quarrel was, and urged
withal Your high displeasure: all this
uttered With gentle breath, calm look,
knees humbly bow'd, Could not take truce
with the unruly spleen Of Tybalt deaf to
peace, but that he tilts With piercing
steel at bold Mercutio's breast, Who all as
hot, turns deadly point to point, And, with
a martial scorn, with one hand beats Cold
death aside, and with the other sends It
back to Tybalt, whose dexterity, Retorts
it: Romeo he cries aloud, 'Hold, friends!
friends, part!' and, swifter than his
tongue, His agile arm beats down their
fatal points, And 'twixt them rushes;
underneath whose arm An envious thrust from
Tybalt hit the life Of stout Mercutio, and
then Tybalt fled; But by and by comes back
to Romeo, Who had but newly entertain'd
revenge, And to 't they go like lightning,
for, ere I Could draw to part them, was
stout Tybalt slain. And, as he fell, did
Romeo turn and fly. This is the truth, or
let Benvolio die.

LADY CAPULET

He is a kinsman to the Montague; Affection makes him false; he speaks not true: Some twenty of them fought in this black strife, And all those twenty could but kill one life. I beg for justice, which thou, prince, must give; Romeo slew Tybalt, Romeo must not live.

PRINCE

Romeo slew him, he slew Mercutio; Who now the price of his dear blood doth owe?

MONTAGUE

Not Romeo, prince, he was Mercutio's friend; His fault concludes but what the law should end, The life of Tybalt.

PRINCE

And for that offence Immediately we do exile him hence: I have an interest in your hate's proceeding, My blood for your rude brawls doth lie a-bleeding; But I'll amerce you with so strong a fine That you shall all repent the loss of mine: I will be deaf to pleading and excuses; Nor tears nor prayers shall purchase out abuses: Therefore use none: let Romeo hence in haste, Else, when he's found, that hour is his last. Bear hence this body and attend our will: Mercy but murders, pardoning those that kill.

Exeunt

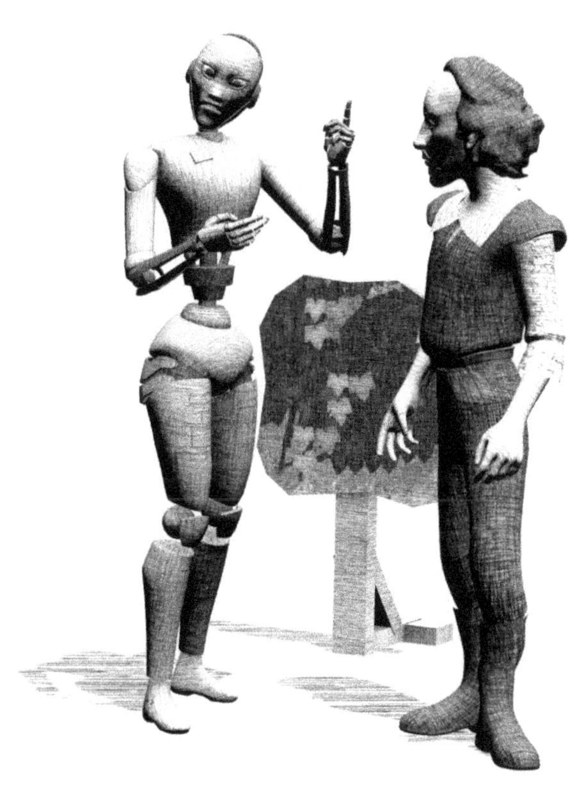

SCENE 2. CAPULET'S ORCHARD.

Enter JULIET

JULIET

Gallop apace, you fiery-footed steeds,
Towards Phoebus' lodging: such a wagoner As
Phaethon would whip you to the west, And
bring in cloudy night immediately. Spread
thy close curtain, love-performing night,
That runaway's eyes may wink and Romeo Leap
to these arms, untalk'd of and unseen.
Lovers can see to do their amorous rites By
their own beauties; or, if love be blind,

It best agrees with night. Come, civil night, Thou sober-suited matron, all in black, And learn me how to lose a winning match, Play'd for a pair of stainless maidenhoods: Hood my unmann'd blood, bating in my cheeks, With thy black mantle; till strange love, grown bold, Think true love acted simple modesty. Come, night; come, Romeo; come, thou day in night; For thou wilt lie upon the wings of night Whiter than new snow on a raven's back. Come, gentle night, come, loving, black-brow'd night, Give me my Romeo; and, when he shall die, Take him and cut him out in little stars, And he will make the face of heaven so fine That all the world will be in love with night And pay no worship to the garish sun. O, I have bought the mansion of a love, But not possess'd it, and, though I am sold, Not yet enjoy'd: so tedious is this day As is the night before some festival To an impatient child that hath new robes And may not wear them. O, here comes my nurse, And she brings news; and every tongue that speaks But Romeo's name speaks heavenly eloquence.

Enter NURSE, with cords

JULIET

Now, nurse, what news? What hast thou there? the cords That Romeo bid thee fetch?

NURSE

Ay, ay, the cords.

Throws them down

JULIET

Ay me! what news? why dost thou wring thy
hands?

NURSE

Ah, well-a-day! he's dead, he's dead, he's
dead! We are undone, lady, we are undone!
Alack the day! he's gone, he's kill'd, he's
dead!

JULIET

Can heaven be so envious?

NURSE

Romeo can, Though heaven cannot: O Romeo,
Romeo! Who ever would have thought it?
Romeo!

JULIET

What devil art thou, that dost torment me
thus? This torture should be roar'd in
dismal hell. Hath Romeo slain himself? say
thou but 'I,' And that bare vowel 'I' shall
poison more Than the death-darting eye of
cockatrice: I am not I, if there be such an
I;
Or those eyes shut, that make thee answer
'I.' If he be slain, say 'I'; or if not,
no: Brief sounds determine of my weal or
woe.

NURSE

I saw the wound, I saw it with mine eyes,—
God save the mark!--here on his manly
breast: A piteous corse, a bloody piteous
corse; Pale, pale as ashes, all bedaub'd in
blood, All in gore-blood; I swounded at the
sight.

JULIET

O, break, my heart! poor bankrupt, break at once! To prison, eyes, ne'er look on liberty! Vile earth, to earth resign; end motion here; And thou and Romeo press one heavy bier!

NURSE

O Tybalt, Tybalt, the best friend I had! O courteous Tybalt! honest gentleman! That ever I should live to see thee dead!

JULIET

What storm is this that blows so contrary? Is Romeo slaughter'd, and is Tybalt dead? My dear-loved cousin, and my dearer lord? Then, dreadful trumpet, sound the general doom! For who is living, if those two are gone?

NURSE

Tybalt is gone, and Romeo banished; Romeo that kill'd him, he is banished.

JULIET

O God! did Romeo's hand shed Tybalt's blood?

NURSE

It did, it did; alas the day, it did!

JULIET

O serpent heart, hid with a flowering face! Did ever dragon keep so fair a cave? Beautiful tyrant! fiend angelical! Dove-feather'd raven! wolvish-ravening lamb! Despised substance of divinest show! Just opposite to what thou justly seem'st, A

damned saint, an honourable villain! O
nature, what hadst thou to do in hell, When
thou didst bower the spirit of a fiend
In moral   of such sweet flesh? Was ever
book containing such vile matter So fairly
bound? O that deceit should dwell In such a
gorgeous palace!

NURSE

There's no trust, No faith, no honesty in
men; all perjured, All forsworn, all
naught, all dissemblers. Ah, where's my
man? give me some aqua vitae: These griefs,
these woes, these sorrows make me old.
Shame come to Romeo!

JULIET

Blister'd be thy tongue
For such a wish! he was not born to shame:
Upon his brow shame is ashamed to sit; For
'tis a throne where honour may be crown'd
Sole monarch of the universal earth. O,
what a beast was I to chide at him!

NURSE

Will you speak well of him that kill'd your
cousin?

JULIET

Shall I speak ill of him that is my
husband? Ah, poor my lord, what tongue
shall smooth thy name, When I, thy three-
hours wife, have mangled it? But,
wherefore, villain, didst thou kill my
cousin? That villain cousin would have
kill'd my husband: Back, foolish tears,
back to your native spring; Your tributary
drops belong to woe, Which you, mistaking,

offer up to joy. My husband lives, that
Tybalt would have slain; And Tybalt's dead,
that would have slain my husband: All this
is comfort; wherefore weep I then? Some
word there was, worser than Tybalt's death,
That murder'd me: I would forget it fain;
But, O, it presses to my memory, Like
damned guilty deeds to sinners' minds:
'Tybalt is dead, and Romeo—banished;' That
'banished,' that one word 'banished,' Hath
slain ten thousand Tybalts. Tybalt's death
Was woe enough, if it had ended there: Or,
if sour woe delights in fellowship And
needly will be rank'd with other griefs,
Why follow'd not, when she said 'Tybalt's
dead,' Thy father, or thy mother, nay, or
both, Which modern lamentations might have
moved? But with a rear-ward following
Tybalt's death, 'Romeo is banished,' to
speak that word, Is father, mother, Tybalt,
Romeo, Juliet, All slain, all dead. 'Romeo
is banished!' There is no end, no limit,
measure, bound, In that word's death; no
words can that woe sound. Where is my
father, and my mother, nurse?

NURSE

Weeping and wailing over Tybalt's corse:
Will you go to them? I will bring you
thither.

JULIET

Wash they his wounds with tears: mine shall
be spent, When theirs are dry, for Romeo's
banishment. Take up those cords: poor
ropes, you are beguiled, Both you and I;
for Romeo is exiled: He made you for a
highway to my bed; But I, a maid, die

maiden-widowed. Come, cords, come, nurse;
I'll to my wedding-bed; And death, not
Romeo, take my maidenhead!

NURSE

Hie to your chamber: I'll find Romeo To
comfort you: I wot well where he is. Hark
ye, your Romeo will be here at night: I'll
to him; he is hid at Laurence' cell.

JULIET

O, find him! give this ring to my true
knight, And bid him come to take his last
farewell.

Exeunt

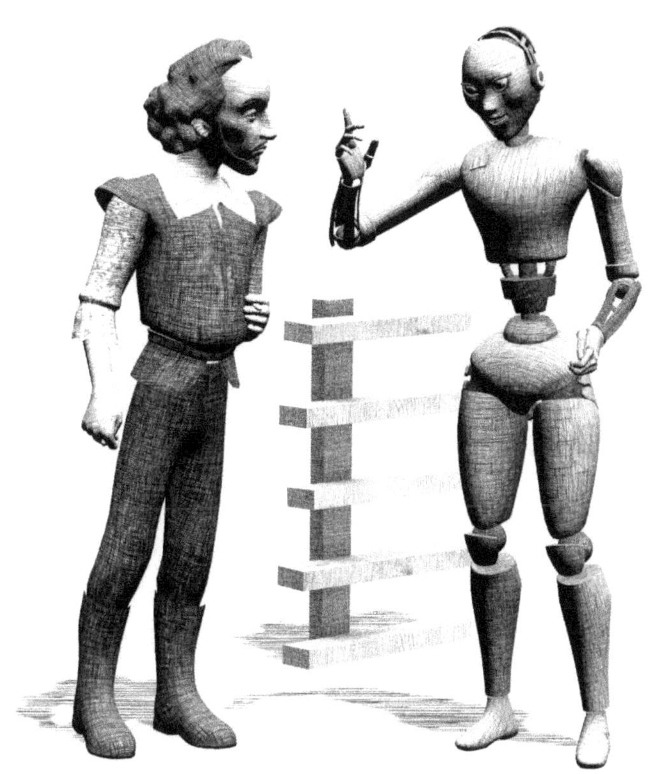

SCENE 3. FRIAR LAURENCE'S CELL.

Enter FRIAR LAURENCE

FRIAR LAURENCE

Romeo, come forth; come forth, thou fearful
man: Affliction is enamour'd of thy parts,
And thou art wedded to calamity.

Enter ROMEO

ROMEO

Father, what news? what is the prince's

doom? What sorrow craves acquaintance at my
hand, That I yet know not?

FRIAR LAURENCE

Too familiar Is my dear son with such sour
company: I bring thee tidings of the
prince's doom.

ROMEO

What less than dooms-day is the prince's
doom?

FRIAR LAURENCE

A gentler judgment vanish'd from his lips,
Not body's death, but body's banishment.

ROMEO

Ha, banishment! be merciful, say 'death;'
For exile hath more terror in his look,
Much more than death: do not say
'banishment.'

FRIAR LAURENCE

Hence from Verona art thou banished: Be
patient, for the world is broad and wide.

ROMEO

There is no world without Verona walls, But
purgatory, torture, hell itself. Hence-
banished is banish'd from the world, And
world's exile is death: then banished, Is
death mis-term'd: calling death banishment,
Thou cutt'st my head off with a golden axe,
And smilest upon the stroke that murders
me.

FRIAR LAURENCE

O deadly sin! O rude unthankfulness! Thy

fault our law calls death; but the kind
prince, Taking thy part, hath rush'd aside
the law, And turn'd that black word death
to banishment: This is dear mercy, and thou
seest it not.

ROMEO

'Tis torture, and not mercy: heaven is
here, Where Juliet lives; and every cat and
dog And little mouse, every unworthy thing,
Live here in heaven and may look on her;
But Romeo may not: more validity, More
honourable state, more courtship lives In
carrion-flies than Romeo: they my seize On
the white wonder of dear Juliet's hand And
steal immortal blessing from her lips, Who
even in pure and vestal modesty, Still
blush, as thinking their own kisses sin;
But Romeo may not; he is banished: Flies
may do this, but I from this must fly: They
are free men, but I am banished. And say'st
thou yet that exile is not death? Hadst
thou no poison mix'd, no sharp-ground
knife, No sudden mean of death, though
ne'er so mean, But 'banished' to kill
me?—'banished'? O friar, the damned use
that word in hell; Howlings attend it: how
hast thou the heart, Being a divine, a
ghostly confessor, A sin-absolver, and my
friend profess'd, To mangle me with that
word 'banished'?

FRIAR LAURENCE
Thou fond mad man, hear me but speak a
word.

ROMEO

O, thou wilt speak again of banishment.

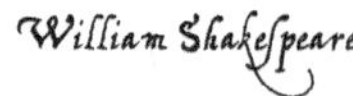

FRIAR LAURENCE

I'll give thee armour to keep off that word:
Adversity's sweet milk, philosophy, To
comfort thee, though thou art banished.

ROMEO

Yet 'banished'? Hang up philosophy! Unless
philosophy can make a Juliet, Displant a
town, reverse a prince's doom, It helps
not, it prevails not: talk no more.

FRIAR LAURENCE

O, then I see that madmen have no ears.

ROMEO

How should they, when that wise men have no
eyes?

FRIAR LAURENCE

Let me dispute with thee of thy estate.

ROMEO

Thou canst not speak of that thou dost not
feel: Wert thou as young as I, Juliet thy
love, An hour but married, Tybalt murdered,
Doting like me and like me banished, Then
mightst thou speak, then mightst thou tear
thy hair, And fall upon the ground, as I do
now, Taking the measure of an unmade grave.

Knocking within

FRIAR LAURENCE

Arise; one knocks; good Romeo, hide
thyself.

ROMEO

Not I; unless the breath of heartsick

groans, Mist-like, infold me from the
search of eyes.

Knocking

FRIAR LAURENCE

Hark, how they knock! Who's there? Romeo,
arise; Thou wilt be taken. Stay awhile!
Stand up;

Knocking

FRIAR LAURENCE

Run to my study. By and by! God's will,
What simpleness is this! I come, I come!

Knocking

FRIAR LAURENCE

Who knocks so hard? whence come you? what's
your will?

NURSE

(Within)
Let me come in, and you shall know my
errand; I come from Lady Juliet.

FRIAR LAURENCE

Welcome, then.

Enter NURSE

NURSE

O holy friar, O, tell me, holy friar, Where
is my lady's lord, where's Romeo?

FRIAR LAURENCE
There on the ground, with his own tears
made drunk.

NURSE

O, he is even in my mistress' case, Just in
her case! O woful sympathy! Piteous
predicament! Even so lies she, Blubbering
and weeping, weeping and blubbering. Stand
up, stand up; stand, and you be a man: For
Juliet's sake, for her sake, rise and
stand; Why should you fall into so deep an
O?

ROMEO

Nurse!

NURSE

Ah sir! ah sir! Well, death's the end of
all.

ROMEO

Spakest thou of Juliet? how is it with her?
Doth she not think me an old murderer, Now
I have stain'd the childhood of our joy
With blood removed but little from her own?
Where is she? and how doth she? and what
says My conceal'd lady to our cancell'd
love?

NURSE

O, she says nothing, sir, but weeps and
weeps; And now falls on her bed; and then
starts up, And Tybalt calls; and then on
Romeo cries, And then down falls again.

ROMEO

As if that name, Shot from the deadly level

of a gun, Did murder her; as that name's
cursed hand Murder'd her kinsman. O, tell
me, friar, tell me, In what vile part of
this anatomy Doth my name lodge? tell me,
that I may sack The hateful mansion.

Drawing his sword

FRIAR LAURENCE
Hold thy desperate hand: Art thou a man?
thy form cries out thou art: Thy tears are
womanish; thy wild acts denote The
unreasonable fury of a beast: Unseemly
woman in a seeming man! Or ill-beseeming
beast in seeming both! Thou hast amazed me:
by my holy order, I thought thy disposition
better temper'd. Hast thou slain Tybalt?
wilt thou slay thyself? And stay thy lady
too that lives in thee, By doing damned
hate upon thyself? Why rail'st thou on thy
birth, the heaven, and earth? Since birth,
and heaven, and earth, all three do meet In
thee at once; which thou at once wouldst
lose. Fie, fie, thou shamest thy shape, thy
love, thy wit; Which, like a usurer,
abound'st in all, And usest none in that
true use indeed Which should bedeck thy
shape, thy love, thy wit: Thy noble shape
is but a form of wax, Digressing from the
valour of a man; Thy dear love sworn but
hollow perjury, Killing that love which
thou hast vow'd to cherish; Thy wit, that
ornament to shape and love, Misshapen in
the conduct of them both, Like powder in a
skitless soldier's flask, Is set afire by
thine own ignorance, And thou dismember'd
with thine own defence. What, rouse thee,
man! thy Juliet is alive, For whose dear

sake thou wast but lately dead; There art
thou happy: Tybalt would kill thee, But
thou slew'st Tybalt; there are thou happy
too: The law that threaten'd death becomes
thy friend And turns it to exile; there art
thou happy: A pack of blessings lights up
upon thy back; Happiness courts thee in her
best array; But, like a misbehaved and
sullen wench, Thou pout'st upon thy fortune
and thy love: Take heed, take heed, for
such die miserable. Go, get thee to thy
love, as was decreed, Ascend her chamber,
hence and comfort her: But look thou stay
not till the watch be set, For then thou
canst not pass to Mantua; Where thou shalt
live, till we can find a time To blaze your
marriage, reconcile your friends, Beg
pardon of the prince, and call thee back
With twenty hundred thousand times more joy
Than thou went'st forth in lamentation. Go
before, nurse: commend me to thy lady; And
bid her hasten all the house to bed, Which
heavy sorrow makes them apt unto: Romeo is
coming.

NURSE

O Lord, I could have stay'd here all the
night To hear good counsel: O, what
learning is! My lord, I'll tell my lady you
will come.

ROMEO

Do so, and bid my sweet prepare to chide.

NURSE

Here, sir, a ring she bid me give you, sir:
Hie you, make haste, for it grows very
late.

Exit

ROMEO

How well my comfort is revived by this!

FRIAR LAURENCE

Go hence; good night; and here stands all
your state: Either be gone before the watch
be set, Or by the break of day disguised
from hence: Sojourn in Mantua; I'll find out
your man, And he shall signify from time to
time Every good hap to you that chances
here: Give me thy hand; 'tis late:
farewell; good night.

ROMEO

But that a joy past joy calls out on me, It
were a grief, so brief to part with thee:
Farewell.

Exeunt

SCENE 4. A ROOM IN CAPULET'S HOUSE.

Enter CAPULET, LADY CAPULET, and PARIS

CAPULET

> Things have fall'n out, sir, so unluckily,
> That we have had no time to move our
> daughter: Look you, she loved her kinsman
> Tybalt dearly, And so did I:--Well, we were
> born to die. 'Tis very late, she'll not
> come down to-night: I promise you, but for
> your company, I would have been a-bed an
> hour ago.

PARIS

These times of woe afford no time to woo.
Madam, good night: commend me to your
daughter.

LADY CAPULET

I will, and know her mind early to-morrow;
To-night she is mew'd up to her heaviness.

CAPULET

Sir Paris, I will make a desperate tender
Of my child's love: I think she will be
ruled In all respects by me; nay, more, I
doubt it not. Wife, go you to her ere you
go to bed; Acquaint her here of my son
Paris' love; And bid her, mark you me, on
Wednesday next— But, soft! what day is
this?

PARIS

Monday, my lord,

CAPULET

Monday! ha, ha! Well, Wednesday is too
soon, O' Thursday let it be: o' Thursday,
tell her, She shall be married to this
noble earl. Will you be ready? do you like
this haste? We'll keep no great ado,--a
friend or two; For, hark you, Tybalt being
slain so late, It may be thought we held
him carelessly, Being our kinsman, if we
revel much: Therefore we'll have some half
a dozen friends, And there an end. But what
say you to Thursday?

PARIS

My lord, I would that Thursday were to-
morrow.

CAPULET

> Well get you gone: o' Thursday be it, then.
> Go you to Juliet ere you go to bed, Prepare
> her, wife, against this wedding-day.
> Farewell, my lord. Light to my chamber, ho!
> Afore me! it is so very very late,
> That we may call it early by and by. Good
> night.

Exeunt

SCENE 5. CAPULET'S ORCHARD.

Enter ROMEO and JULIET above, at the window

JULIET

> Wilt thou be gone? it is not yet near day:
> It was the nightingale, and not the lark,
> That pierced the fearful hollow of thine
> ear; Nightly she sings on yon pomegranate-
> tree: Believe me, love, it was the
> nightingale.

ROMEO

> It was the lark, the herald of the morn, No

nightingale: look, love, what envious
streaks Do lace the severing clouds in
yonder east: Night's candles are burnt out,
and jocund day Stands tiptoe on the misty
mountain tops. I must be gone and live, or
stay and die.

JULIET

Yon light is not day-light, I know it, I:
It is some meteor that the sun exhales, To
be to thee this night a torch-bearer, And
light thee on thy way to Mantua: Therefore
stay yet; thou need'st not to be gone.

ROMEO

Let me be ta'en, let me be put to death; I
am content, so thou wilt have it so. I'll
say yon grey is not the morning's eye, 'Tis
but the pale reflex of Cynthia's brow; Nor
that is not the lark, whose notes do beat
The vaulty heaven so high above our heads:
I have more care to stay than will to go:
Come, death, and welcome! Juliet wills it
so. How is't, my soul? let's talk; it is
not day.

JULIET

It is, it is: hie hence, be gone, away! It
is the lark that sings so out of tune,
Straining harsh discords and unpleasing
sharps. Some say the lark makes sweet
division; This doth not so, for she
divideth us: Some say the lark and loathed
toad change eyes, O, now I would they had
changed voices too! Since arm from arm that
voice doth us affray, Hunting thee hence
with hunt's-up to the day, O, now be gone;
more light and light it grows.

ROMEO

> More light and light; more dark and dark
> our woes!

Enter NURSE, to the chamber

NURSE

> Madam!

JULIET

> Nurse?

NURSE

> Your lady mother is coming to your chamber:
> The day is broke; be wary, look about.

Exit

JULIET

> Then, window, let day in, and let life out.

ROMEO

> Farewell, farewell! one kiss, and I'll
> descend.

He goeth down

JULIET

> Art thou gone so? love, lord, ay, husband,
> friend! I must hear from thee every day in
> the hour, For in a minute there are many
> days: O, by this count I shall be much in
> years Ere I again behold my Romeo!

ROMEO

> Farewell! I will omit no opportunity That
> may convey my greetings, love, to thee.

JULIET

O think'st thou we shall ever meet again?

ROMEO

I doubt it not; and all these woes shall serve For sweet discourses in our time to come.

JULIET

O God, I have an ill-divining soul! Methinks I see thee, now thou art below, As one dead in the bottom of a tomb: Either my eyesight fails, or thou look'st pale.

ROMEO

And trust me, love, in my eye so do you: Dry sorrow drinks our blood. Adieu, adieu!

Exit

JULIET

O fortune, fortune! all men call thee fickle: If thou art fickle, what dost thou with him. That is renown'd for faith? Be fickle, fortune; For then, I hope, thou wilt not keep him long, But send him back.

LADY CAPULET

(Within)
Ho, daughter! are you up?

JULIET

Who is't that calls? is it my lady mother? Is she not down so late, or up so early? What unaccustom'd cause procures her hither?

Enter LADY CAPULET

LADY CAPULET

Why, how now, Juliet!

JULIET

Madam, I am not well.

LADY CAPULET

Evermore weeping for your cousin's death?
What, wilt thou wash him from his grave
with tears? An if thou couldst, thou
couldst not make him live; Therefore, have
done: some grief shows much of love; But
much of grief shows still some want of wit.

JULIET

Yet let me weep for such a feeling loss.

LADY CAPULET

So shall you feel the loss, but not the
friend Which you weep for.

JULIET

Feeling so the loss, Cannot choose but ever
weep the friend.

LADY CAPULET

Well, girl, thou weep'st not so much for
his death, As that the villain lives which
slaughter'd him.

JULIET

What villain madam?

LADY CAPULET

That same villain, Romeo.

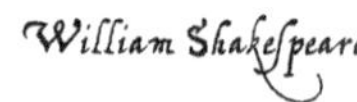

JULIET

(Aside)
Villain and he be many miles asunder.— God
Pardon him! I do, with all my heart; And
yet no man like he doth grieve my heart.

LADY CAPULET

That is, because the traitor murderer
lives.

JULIET

Ay, madam, from the reach of these my
hands: Would none but I might venge my
cousin's death!

LADY CAPULET

We will have vengeance for it, fear thou
not: Then weep no more. I'll send to one in
Mantua, Where that same banish'd runagate
doth live, Shall give him such an
unaccustom'd dram, That he shall soon keep
Tybalt company: And then, I hope, thou wilt
be satisfied.

JULIET

Indeed, I never shall be satisfied
With Romeo, till I behold him—dead-- Is my
poor heart for a kinsman vex'd. Madam, if
you could find out but a man To bear a
poison, I would temper it; That Romeo
should, upon receipt thereof, Soon sleep in
quiet. O, how my heart abhors To hear him
named, and cannot come to him. To wreak the
love I bore my cousin
Upon his body that slaughter'd him!

LADY CAPULET

Find thou the means, and I'll find such a

man. But now I'll tell thee joyful tidings,
girl.

JULIET

And joy comes well in such a needy time:
What are they, I beseech your ladyship?

LADY CAPULET

Well, well, thou hast a careful father,
child; One who, to put thee from thy
heaviness, Hath sorted out a sudden day of
joy, That thou expect'st not nor I look'd
not for.

JULIET

Madam, in happy time, what day is that?

LADY CAPULET

Marry, my child, early next Thursday morn,
The gallant, young and noble gentleman, The
County Paris, at Saint Peter's Church,
Shall happily make thee there a joyful
bride.

JULIET

Now, by Saint Peter's Church and Peter too,
He shall not make me there a joyful bride.
I wonder at this haste; that I must wed Ere
he, that should be husband, comes to woo. I
pray you, tell my lord and father, madam, I
will not marry yet; and, when I do, I
swear, It shall be Romeo, whom you know I
hate, Rather than Paris. These are news
indeed!

LADY CAPULET

Here comes your father; tell him so

yourself, And see how he will take it at
your hands.

Enter CAPULET and NURSE

CAPULET

When the sun sets, the air doth drizzle
dew; But for the sunset of my brother's son
It rains downright. How now! a conduit,
girl? what, still in tears? Evermore
showering? In one little body Thou
counterfeit'st a bark, a sea, a wind; For
still thy eyes, which I may call the sea,
Do ebb and flow with tears; the bark thy
body is, Sailing in this salt flood; the
winds, thy sighs; Who, raging with thy
tears, and they with them, Without a sudden
calm, will overset Thy tempest-tossed body.
How now, wife! Have you deliver'd to her
our decree?

LADY CAPULET

Ay, sir; but she will none, she gives you
thanks. I would the fool were married to
her grave!

CAPULET

Soft! take me with you, take me with you,
wife. How! will she none? doth she not give
us thanks? Is she not proud? doth she not
count her blest, Unworthy as she is, that
we have wrought So worthy a gentleman to be
her bridegroom?

JULIET

Not proud, you have; but thankful, that you
have: Proud can I never be of what I hate;

But thankful even for hate, that is meant
love.

CAPULET

How now, how now, chop-logic! What is this?
'Proud,' and 'I thank you,' and 'I thank
you not;' And yet 'not proud,' mistress
minion, you, Thank me no thankings, nor,
proud me no prouds, But fettle your fine
joints 'gainst Thursday next, To go with
Paris to Saint Peter's Church, Or I will
drag thee on a hurdle thither. Out, you
green-sickness carrion! out, you baggage!
You tallow-face!

LADY CAPULET

Fie, fie! what, are you mad?

JULIET

Good father, I beseech you on my knees,
Hear me with patience but to speak a word.

CAPULET

Hang thee, young baggage! disobedient
wretch! I tell thee what: get thee to
church o' Thursday, Or never after look me
in the face: Speak not, reply not, do not
answer me; My fingers itch. Wife, we scarce
thought us blest That God had lent us but
this only child; But now I see this one is
one too much, And that we have a curse in
having her: Out on her, hilding!

NURSE

God in heaven bless her! You are to blame,
my lord, to rate her so.

CAPULET

And why, my lady wisdom? hold your tongue,
Good prudence; smatter with your gossips,
go.

NURSE

I speak no treason.

CAPULET

O, God ye god-den.

NURSE

May not one speak?

CAPULET

Peace, you mumbling fool! Utter your
gravity o'er a gossip's bowl; For here we
need it not.

LADY CAPULET

You are too hot.

CAPULET

God's bread! it makes me mad: Day, night,
hour, tide, time, work, play, Alone, in
company, still my care hath been To have
her match'd: and having now provided A
gentleman of noble parentage, Of fair
demesnes, youthful, and nobly train'd,
Stuff'd, as they say, with honourable parts,
Proportion'd as one's thought would wish a
man; And then to have a wretched puling
fool, A whining mammet, in her fortune's
tender, To answer 'I'll not wed; I cannot
love, I am too young; I pray you, pardon
me.' But, as you will not wed, I'll pardon
you: Graze where you will you shall not
house with me: Look to't, think on't, I do

not use to jest. Thursday is near; lay hand
on heart, advise: An you be mine, I'll give
you to my friend; And you be not, hang,
beg, starve, die in the streets, For, by my
soul, I'll ne'er acknowledge thee, Nor what
is mine shall never do thee good: Trust
to't, bethink you; I'll not be forsworn.

Exit

JULIET

Is there no pity sitting in the clouds,
That sees into the bottom of my grief? O,
sweet my mother, cast me not away! Delay
this marriage for a month, a week; Or, if
you do not, make the bridal bed In that dim
monument where Tybalt lies.

LADY CAPULET

Talk not to me, for I'll not speak a word:
Do as thou wilt, for I have done with thee.

Exit

JULIET

O God!--O nurse, how shall this be
prevented? My husband is on earth, my faith
in heaven; How shall that faith return
again to earth, Unless that husband send it
me from heaven By leaving earth? comfort
me, counsel me. Alack, alack, that heaven
should practise stratagems Upon so soft a
subject as myself! What say'st thou? hast
thou not a word of joy? Some comfort,
nurse.

NURSE

Faith, here it is. Romeo is banish'd; and

all the world to nothing, That he dares ne'er come back to challenge you; Or, if he do, it needs must be by stealth. Then, since the case so stands as now it doth, I think it best you married with the county. O, he's a lovely gentleman! Romeo's a dishclout to him: an eagle, madam, Hath not so green, so quick, so fair an eye As Paris hath. Beshrew my very heart, I think you are happy in this second match, For it excels your first: or if it did not, Your first is dead; or 'twere as good he were, As living here and you no use of him.

JULIET

Speakest thou from thy heart?

NURSE

And from my soul too; Or else beshrew them both.

JULIET

Amen!

NURSE

What?

JULIET

Well, thou hast comforted me marvellous much. Go in: and tell my lady I am gone, Having displeased my father, to Laurence' cell, To make confession and to be absolved.

NURSE

Marry, I will; and this is wisely done.

Exit

JULIET

> Ancient damnation! O most wicked fiend! Is
> it more sin to wish me thus forsworn, Or to
> dispraise my lord with that same tongue
> Which she hath praised him with above
> compare So many thousand times? Go,
> counsellor; Thou and my bosom henceforth
> shall be twain. I'll to the friar, to know
> his remedy: If all else fail, myself have
> power to die.

Exit

ACT IV

SCENE 1. FRIAR LAURENCE'S CELL.

Enter FRIAR LAURENCE and PARIS

FRIAR LAURENCE
>   On Thursday, sir? the time is very short.

PARIS
>   My father Capulet will have it so; And I am
>   nothing slow to slack his haste.

FRIAR LAURENCE

You say you do not know the lady's mind:
Uneven is the course, I like it not.

PARIS

Immoderately she weeps for Tybalt's death,
And therefore have I little talk'd of love;
For Venus smiles not in a house of tears.
Now, sir, her father counts it dangerous
That she doth give her sorrow so much sway,
And in his wisdom hastes our marriage, To
stop the inundation of her tears; Which,
too much minded by herself alone, May be
put from her by society: Now do you know
the reason of this haste.

FRIAR LAURENCE

(Aside)
I would I knew not why it should be slow'd.
Look, sir, here comes the lady towards my
cell.

Enter JULIET

PARIS

Happily met, my lady and my wife!

JULIET

That may be, sir, when I may be a wife.

PARIS

That may be must be, love, on Thursday
next.

JULIET

What must be shall be.

FRIAR LAURENCE

That's a certain text.

PARIS

Come you to make confession to this father?

JULIET

To answer that, I should confess to you.

PARIS

Do not deny to him that you love me.

JULIET

I will confess to you that I love him.

PARIS

So will ye, I am sure, that you love me.

JULIET

If I do so, it will be of more price, Being
spoke behind your back, than to your face.

PARIS

Poor soul, thy face is much abused with
tears.

JULIET

The tears have got small victory by that;
For it was bad enough before their spite.

PARIS

Thou wrong'st it, more than tears, with
that report.

JULIET

That is no slander, sir, which is a truth;
And what I spake, I spake it to my face.

PARIS

Thy face is mine, and thou hast slander'd it.

JULIET

It may be so, for it is not mine own. Are you at leisure, holy father, now; Or shall I come to you at evening mass?

FRIAR LAURENCE

My leisure serves me, pensive daughter, now. My lord, we must entreat the time alone.

PARIS

God shield I should disturb devotion! Juliet, on Thursday early will I rouse ye: Till then, adieu; and keep this holy kiss.

Exit

JULIET

O shut the door! and when thou hast done so, Come weep with me; past hope, past cure, past help!

FRIAR LAURENCE

Ah, Juliet, I already know thy grief; It strains me past the compass of my wits: I hear thou must, and nothing may prorogue it, On Thursday next be married to this county.

JULIET

Tell me not, friar, that thou hear'st of this, Unless thou tell me how I may prevent it: If, in thy wisdom, thou canst give no help, Do thou but call my resolution wise,

And with this knife I'll help it presently.
God join'd my heart and Romeo's, thou our
hands; And ere this hand, by thee to Romeo
seal'd, Shall be the label to another deed,
Or my true heart with treacherous revolt
Turn to another, this shall slay them both:
Therefore, out of thy long-experienced
time, Give me some present counsel, or,
behold, 'Twixt my extremes and me this
bloody knife Shall play the umpire,
arbitrating that Which the commission of
thy years and art Could to no issue of true
honour bring. Be not so long to speak; I
long to die, If what thou speak'st speak
not of remedy.

FRIAR LAURENCE

Hold, daughter: I do spy a kind of hope,
Which craves as desperate an execution. As
that is desperate which we would prevent.
If, rather than to marry County Paris, Thou
hast the strength of will to slay thyself,
Then is it likely thou wilt undertake A
thing like death to chide away this shame,
That copest with death himself to scape
from it: And, if thou darest, I'll give
thee remedy.

JULIET

O, bid me leap, rather than marry Paris,
From off the battlements of yonder tower; Or
walk in thievish ways; or bid me lurk Where
serpents are; chain me with roaring bears;
Or shut me nightly in a charnel-house,
O'er-cover'd quite with dead men's rattling
bones, With reeky shanks and yellow
chapless skulls; Or bid me go into a new-
made grave And hide me with a dead man in

his shroud; Things that, to hear them told,
have made me tremble; And I will do it
without fear or doubt, To live an unstain'd
wife to my sweet love.

FRIAR LAURENCE

Hold, then; go home, be merry, give consent
To marry Paris: Wednesday is to-morrow: To-
morrow night look that thou lie alone; Let
not thy nurse lie with thee in thy chamber:
Take thou this vial, being then in bed, And
this distilled liquor drink thou off; When
presently through all thy veins shall run A
cold and drowsy humour, for no pulse Shall
keep his native progress, but surcease: No
warmth, no breath, shall testify thou
livest; The roses in thy lips and cheeks
shall fade To paly ashes, thy eyes' windows
fall, Like death, when he shuts up the day
of life; Each part, deprived of supple
government, Shall, stiff and stark and cold,
appear like death: And in this borrow'd
likeness of shrunk death Thou shalt
continue two and forty hours, And then
awake as from a pleasant sleep. Now, when
the bridegroom in the morning comes To
rouse thee from thy bed, there art thou
dead: Then, as the manner of our country
is, In thy best robes uncover'd on the bier
Thou shalt be borne to that same ancient
vault Where all the kindred of the Capulets
lie. In the mean time, against thou shalt
awake, Shall Romeo by my letters know our
drift, And hither shall he come: and he and
I Will watch thy waking, and that very
night Shall Romeo bear thee hence to
Mantua. And this shall free thee from this
present shame; If no inconstant toy, nor

womanish fear, Abate thy valour in the
acting it.

JULIET

Give me, give me! O, tell not me of fear!

FRIAR LAURENCE

Hold; get you gone, be strong and
prosperous In this resolve: I'll send a
friar with speed To Mantua, with my letters
to thy lord.

JULIET

Love give me strength! and strength shall
help afford. Farewell, dear father!

Exeunt

SCENE 2. HALL IN CAPULET'S HOUSE.

Enter CAPULET, LADY CAPULET, Nurse, and two
SERVINGMEN

CAPULET

So many guests invite as here are writ.

Exit FIRSE SERVENT

CAPULET

Sirrah, go hire me twenty cunning cooks.

SECOND SERVANT

>You shall have none ill, sir; for I'll try
>if they can lick their fingers.

CAPULET

>How canst thou try them so? Second Servant
>Marry, sir, 'tis an ill cook that cannot
>lick his own fingers: therefore he that
>cannot lick his fingers goes not with me.

CAPULET

>Go, be gone.

Exit SECOND SERVENT

CAPULET

>We shall be much unfurnished for this time.
>What, is my daughter gone to Friar
>Laurence?

NURSE

>Ay, forsooth.

CAPULET

>Well, he may chance to do some good on her:
>A peevish self-will'd harlotry it is.

NURSE

>See where she comes from shrift with merry
>look.

Enter JULIET

CAPULET

>How now, my headstrong! where have you been
>gadding?

JULIET

Where I have learn'd me to repent the sin
Of disobedient opposition
To you and your behests, and am enjoin'd By
holy Laurence to fall prostrate here, And
beg your pardon: pardon, I beseech you!
Henceforward I am ever ruled by you.

CAPULET

Send for the county; go tell him of this:
I'll have this knot knit up to-morrow
morning.

JULIET

I met the youthful lord at Laurence' cell;
And gave him what becomed love I might, Not
step o'er the bounds of modesty.

CAPULET

Why, I am glad on't; this is well: stand
up: This is as't should be. Let me see the
county; Ay, marry, go, I say, and fetch him
hither. Now, afore God! this reverend holy
friar, Our whole city is much bound to him.

JULIET

Nurse, will you go with me into my closet,
To help me sort such needful ornaments As
you think fit to furnish me to-morrow?

LADY CAPULET

No, not till Thursday; there is time
enough.

CAPULET

Go, nurse, go with her: we'll to church to-
morrow.

Exeunt JULIET and NURSE

LADY CAPULET

> We shall be short in our provision: 'Tis
> now near night.

CAPULET

> Tush, I will stir about, And all things
> shall be well, I warrant thee, wife: Go
> thou to Juliet, help to deck up her; I'll
> not to bed to-night; let me alone; I'll
> play the housewife for this once. What, ho!
> They are all forth. Well, I will walk
> myself To County Paris, to prepare him up
> Against to-morrow: my heart is wondrous
> light, Since this same wayward girl is so
> reclaim'd.

Exeunt

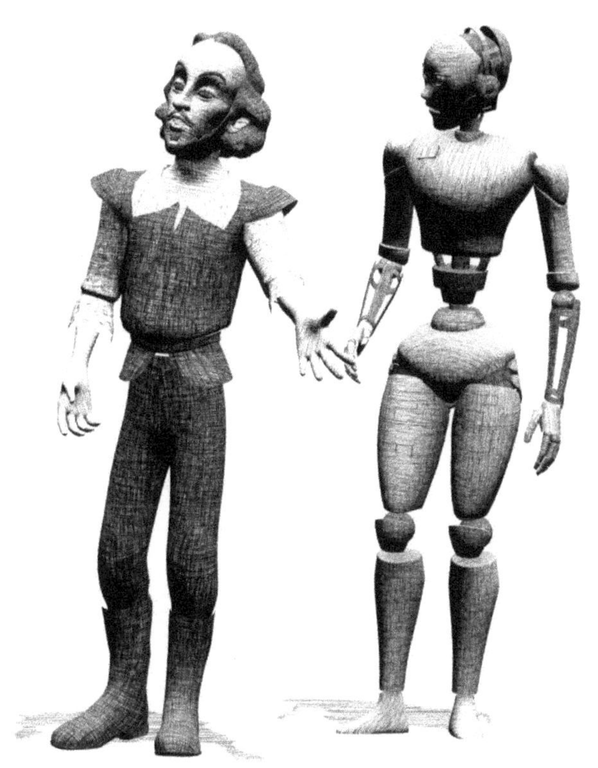

SCENE 3. JULIET'S CHAMBER.

Enter JULIET and NURSE

JULIET

>   Ay, those attires are best: but, gentle
>   nurse, I pray thee, leave me to my self to-
>   night, For I have need of many orisons To
>   move the heavens to smile upon my state,
>   Which, well thou know'st, is cross, and
>   full of sin.

Enter LADY CAPULET

LADY CAPULET

>What, are you busy, ho? need you my help?

JULIET

>No, madam; we have cull'd such necessaries
>As are behoveful for our state to-morrow:
>So please you, let me now be left alone,
>And let the nurse this night sit up with
>you; For, I am sure, you have your hands
>full all, In this so sudden business.

LADY CAPULET

>Good night: Get thee to bed, and rest; for
>thou hast need.

Exeunt LADY CAPULET and NURSE

JULIET

>Farewell! God knows when we shall meet
>again. I have a faint cold fear thrills
>through my veins, That almost freezes up
>the heat of life: I'll call them back again
>to comfort me: Nurse! What should she do
>here? My dismal scene I needs must act
>alone. Come, vial. What if this mixture do
>not work at all? Shall I be married then
>to-morrow morning? No, no: this shall
>forbid it: lie thou there.

Laying down her dagger

JULIET

>What if it be a poison, which the friar
>Subtly hath minister'd to have me dead,
>Lest in this marriage he should be
>dishonour'd, Because he married me before
>to Romeo? I fear it is: and yet, methinks,
>it should not, For he hath still been tried

a holy man. How if, when I am laid into the
tomb, I wake before the time that Romeo
Come to redeem me? there's a fearful point!
Shall I not, then, be stifled in the vault,
To whose foul mouth no healthsome air
breathes in, And there die strangled ere my
Romeo comes? Or, if I live, is it not very
like, The horrible conceit of death and
night, Together with the terror of the
place,— As in a vault, an ancient
receptacle, Where, for these many hundred
years, the bones Of all my buried ancestors
are packed: Where bloody Tybalt, yet but
green in earth, Lies festering in his
shroud; where, as they say, At some hours
in the night spirits resort;— Alack, alack,
is it not like that I, So early waking,
what with loathsome smells, And shrieks
like mandrakes' torn out of the earth, That
living mortals, hearing them, run mad:— O,
if I wake, shall I not be distraught,
Environed with all these hideous fears? And
madly play with my forefather's joints? And
pluck the mangled Tybalt from his shroud?
And, in this rage, with some great
kinsman's bone, As with a club, dash out my
desperate brains? O, look! methinks I see
my cousin's ghost Seeking out Romeo, that
did spit his body Upon a rapier's point:
stay, Tybalt, stay! Romeo, I come! this do
I drink to thee.

She falls upon her bed, within the curtains.

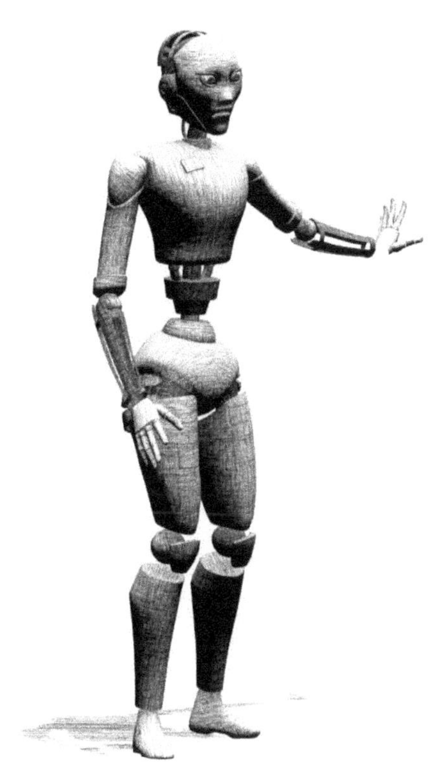

SCENE 4. HALL IN CAPULET'S HOUSE.

Enter LADY CAPULET and Nurse

LADY CAPULET

    Hold, take these keys, and fetch more
    spices, nurse.

NURSE

    They call for dates and quinces in the
    pastry.

Enter CAPULET

CAPULET

> Come, stir, stir, stir! the second cock
> hath crow'd, The curfew-bell hath rung,
> 'tis three o'clock: Look to the baked
> meats, good Angelica: Spare not for the
> cost.

NURSE

> Go, you cot-quean, go, Get you to bed;
> faith, You'll be sick to-morrow For this
> night's watching.

CAPULET

> No, not a whit: what! I have watch'd ere
> now All night for lesser cause, and ne'er
> been sick.

LADY CAPULET

> Ay, you have been a mouse-hunt in your
> time; But I will watch you from such
> watching now.

Exeunt LADY CAPULET and NURSE

CAPULET

> A jealous hood, a jealous hood!

*Enter three or four SERVINGMEN, with spits, logs,
and baskets*

CAPULET

> Now, fellow, What's there?

FIRST SERVANT

> Things for the cook, sir; but I know not
> what.

CAPULET

    Make haste, make haste.

Exit FIRST SERVENT

    Sirrah, fetch drier logs: Call Peter, he will show thee where they are. Second Servant I have a head, sir, that will find out logs, And never trouble Peter for the matter.

Exit

CAPULET

    Mass, and well said; a merry whoreson, ha! Thou shalt be logger-head. Good faith, 'tis day: The county will be here with music straight, For so he said he would: I hear him near.

Music within

CAPULET

    Nurse! Wife! What, ho! What, nurse, I say!

Re-enter NURSE

CAPULET

    Go waken Juliet, go and trim her up; I'll go and chat with Paris: hie, make haste, Make haste; the bridegroom he is come already: Make haste, I say.

Exeunt

SCENE 5. JULIET'S CHAMBER.

Enter NURSE

NURSE

Mistress! what, mistress! Juliet! fast, I
warrant her, she: Why, lamb! why, lady! fie,
you slug-a-bed! Why, love, I say! madam!
sweet-heart! why, bride! What, not a word?
you take your pennyworths now; Sleep for a
week; for the next night, I warrant, The
County Paris hath set up his rest, That you
shall rest but little. God forgive me,
Marry, and amen, how sound is she asleep! I

William Shakespeare

must needs wake her. Madam, madam, madam!
Ay, let the county take you in your bed;
He'll fright you up, i' faith. Will it not
be?

Undraws the curtains

NURSE

What, dress'd! and in your clothes! and
down again! I must needs wake you; Lady!
lady! lady! Alas, alas! Help, help! my
lady's dead! O, well-a-day, that ever I was
born! Some aqua vitae, ho! My lord! my
lady!

Enter LADY CAPULET

LADY CAPULET

What noise is here?

NURSE

O lamentable day!

LADY CAPULET

What is the matter?

NURSE

Look, look! O heavy day!

LADY CAPULET

O me, O me! My child, my only life, Revive,
look up, or I will die with thee! Help,
help! Call help.

Enter CAPULET

CAPULET

> For shame, bring Juliet forth; her lord is
> come.

NURSE

> She's dead, deceased, she's dead; alack the
> day!

LADY CAPULET

> Alack the day, she's dead, she's dead,
> she's dead!

CAPULET

> Ha! let me see her: out, alas! she's cold:
> Her blood is settled, and her joints are
> stiff; Life and these lips have long been
> separated: Death lies on her like an
> untimely frost Upon the sweetest flower of
> all the field.

NURSE

> O lamentable day!

LADY CAPULET

> O woful time!

CAPULET

> Death, that hath ta'en her hence to make me
> wail, Ties up my tongue, and will not let
> me speak.

Enter FRIAR LAURENCE and PARIS, with Musicians

FRIAR LAURENCE

> Come, is the bride ready to go to church?

CAPULET

> Ready to go, but never to return. O son!

the night before thy wedding-day Hath Death
lain with thy wife. There she lies, Flower
as she was, deflowered by him. Death is my
son-in-law, Death is my heir; My daughter
he hath wedded: I will die, And leave him
all; life, living, all is Death's.

PARIS

Have I thought long to see this morning's
face, And doth it give me such a sight as
this?

LADY CAPULET

Accursed, unhappy, wretched, hateful day!
Most miserable hour that e'er time saw In
lasting labour of his pilgrimage! But one,
poor one, one poor and loving child, But
one thing to rejoice and solace in, And
cruel death hath catch'd it from my sight!

NURSE

O woe! O woful, woful, woful day! Most
lamentable day, most woful day, That ever,
ever, I did yet behold! O day! O day! O
day! O hateful day! Never was seen so black
a day as this: O woful day, O woful day!

PARIS

Beguiled, divorced, wronged, spited, slain!
Most detestable death, by thee beguil'd, By
cruel cruel thee quite overthrown! O love!
O life! not life, but love in death!

CAPULET

Despised, distressed, hated, martyr'd,
kill'd! Uncomfortable time, why camest thou
now To murder, murder our solemnity? O
child! O child! my soul, and not my child!

Dead art thou! Alack! my child is dead; And
with my child my joys are buried.

FRIAR LAURENCE

Peace, ho, for shame! confusion's cure
lives not In these confusions. Heaven and
yourself Had part in this fair maid; now
heaven hath all, And all the better is it
for the maid: Your part in her you could
not keep from death, But heaven keeps his
part in eternal life. The most you sought
was her promotion; For 'twas your heaven
she should be advanced: And weep ye now,
seeing she is advanced Above the clouds, as
high as heaven itself? O, in this love, you
love your child so ill, That you run mad,
seeing that she is well: She's not well
married that lives married long; But she's
best married that dies married young. Dry
up your tears, and stick your rosemary On
this fair corse; and, as the custom is, In
all her best array bear her to church: For
though fond nature bids us an lament, Yet
nature's tears are reason's merriment.

CAPULET

All things that we ordained festival, Turn
from their office to black funeral; Our
instruments to melancholy bells, Our
wedding cheer to a sad burial feast, Our
solemn hymns to sullen dirges change, Our
bridal flowers serve for a buried corse, And
all things change them to the contrary.

FRIAR LAURENCE

Sir, go you in; and, madam, go with him;
And go, Sir Paris; every one prepare To
follow this fair corse unto her grave: The

William Shakespeare

heavens do lour upon you for some ill; Move
them no more by crossing their high will.

*Exeunt CAPULET, LADY CAPULET, PARIS, and FRIAR
LAURENCE*

FIRST MUSICIAN

Faith, we may put up our pipes, and be
gone.

NURSE

Honest goodfellows, ah, put up, put up;
For, well you know, this is a pitiful case.

Exit

FIRST MUSICIAN

Ay, by my troth, the case may be amended.

Enter PETER

PETER

Musicians, O, musicians, 'Heart's ease,
Heart's ease:' O, an you will have me live,
play 'Heart's ease.'

FIRST MUSICIAN

Why 'Heart's ease?'

PETER

O, musicians, because my heart itself plays
'My heart is full of woe:' O, play me some
merry dump, to comfort me.

FIRST MUSICIAN

Not a dump we; 'tis no time to play now.

PETER

You will not, then?

FIRST MUSICIAN

No.

PETER

I will then give it you soundly.

FIRST MUSICIAN

What will you give us?

PETER

No money, on my faith, but the gleek; I
will give you the minstrel.

FIRST MUSICIAN

Then I will give you the serving-creature.

PETER

Then will I lay the serving-creature's
dagger on your pate. I will carry no
crotchets: I'll re you, I'll fa you; do you
note me?

FIRST MUSICIAN

An you re us and fa us, you note us.

SECOND MUSICIAN

Pray you, put up your dagger, and put out
your wit.

PETER

Then have at you with my wit! I will drybeat you with an iron wit, and put up my
iron dagger. Answer me like men: 'When
griping grief the heart doth wound, And
doleful dumps the mind oppress, Then music

with her silver sound'-- why 'silver
sound'? why 'music with her silver sound'?
What say you, Simon Catling?

MUSICIAN

Marry, sir, because silver hath a sweet
sound.

PETER

Pretty! What say you, Hugh Rebeck?

SECOND MUSICIAN

I say 'silver sound,' because musicians
sound for silver.

PETER

Pretty too! What say you, James Soundpost?

THIRD MUSICIAN

Faith, I know not what to say.

PETER

O, I cry you mercy; you are the singer: I
will say for you. It is 'music with her
silver sound,' because musicians have no
gold for sounding: 'Then music with her
silver sound With speedy help doth lend
redress.'

Exit

FIRST MUSICIAN

What a pestilent knave is this same!

SECOND MUSICIAN

Hang him, Jack! Come, we'll in here; tarry
for the mourners, and stay dinner.

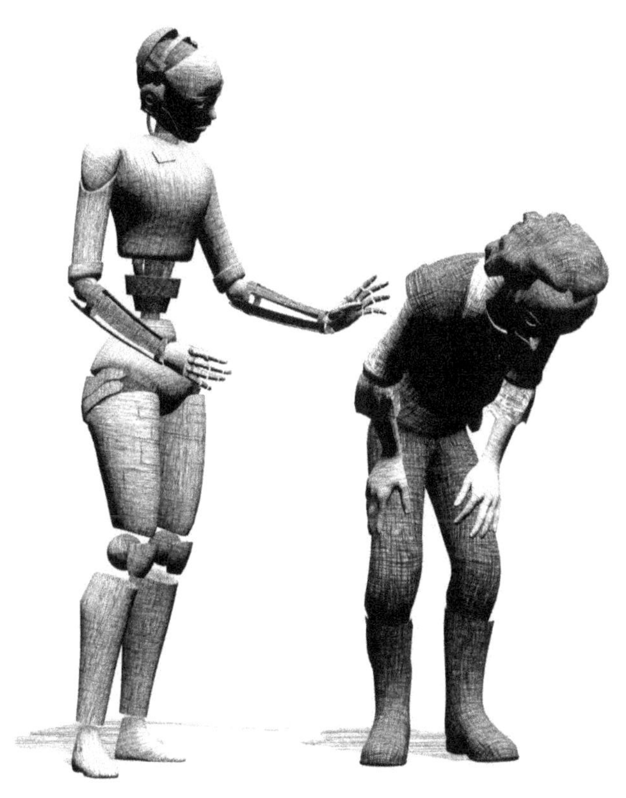

ACT V

SCENE 1. MANTUA. A STREET.

Enter ROMEO

ROMEO

>If I may trust the flattering truth of sleep, My dreams presage some joyful news at hand: My bosom's lord sits lightly in his throne; And all this day an unaccustom'd spirit Lifts me above the ground with cheerful thoughts. I dreamt my

lady came and found me dead— Strange dream,
that gives a dead man leave to think!— And
breathed such life with kisses in my lips,
That I revived, and was an emperor. Ah me!
how sweet is love itself possess'd, When
but love's shadows are so rich in joy!

Enter BALTHASAR, booted

ROMEO

News from Verona!--How now, Balthasar! Dost
thou not bring me letters from the friar?
How doth my lady? Is my father well? How
fares my Juliet? that I ask again; For
nothing can be ill, if she be well.

BALTHASAR

Then she is well, and nothing can be ill:
Her body sleeps in Capel's monument, And
her immortal part with angels lives. I saw
her laid low in her kindred's vault, And
presently took post to tell it you: O,
pardon me for bringing these ill news,
Since you did leave it for my office, sir.

ROMEO

Is it even so? then I defy you, stars! Thou
know'st my lodging: get me ink and paper,
And hire post-horses; I will hence to-
night.

BALTHASAR

I do beseech you, sir, have patience: Your
looks are pale and wild, and do import Some
misadventure.

ROMEO

Tush, thou art deceived: Leave me, and do

the thing I bid thee do. Hast thou no letters to me from the friar?

BALTHASAR

No, my good lord.

ROMEO

No matter: get thee gone, And hire those horses; I'll be with thee straight.

Exit BALTHASAR

ROMEO

Well, Juliet, I will lie with thee to-night. Let's see for means: O mischief, thou art swift To enter in the thoughts of desperate men! I do remember an apothecary,— And hereabouts he dwells,-- which late I noted In tatter'd weeds, with overwhelming brows, Culling of simples; meagre were his looks, Sharp misery had worn him to the bones: And in his needy shop a tortoise hung, An alligator stuff'd, and other skins Of ill-shaped fishes; and about his shelves A beggarly account of empty boxes,
Green earthen pots, bladders and musty seeds, Remnants of packthread and old cakes of roses, Were thinly scatter'd, to make up a show. Noting this penury, to myself I said 'An if a man did need a poison now, Whose sale is present death in Mantua, Here lives a caitiff wretch would sell it him.' O, this same thought did but forerun my need; And this same needy man must sell it me. As I remember, this should be the house. Being holiday, the beggar's shop is shut. What, ho! apothecary!

Enter APOTHECARY

APOTHECARY

Who calls so loud?

ROMEO

Come hither, man. I see that thou art poor:
Hold, there is forty ducats: let me have A
dram of poison, such soon-speeding gear As
will disperse itself through all the veins
That the life-weary taker may fall dead And
that the trunk may be discharged of breath
As violently as hasty powder fired Doth
hurry from the fatal cannon's womb.

APOTHECARY

Such mortal drugs I have; but Mantua's law
Is death to any he that utters them.

ROMEO

Art thou so bare and full of wretchedness,
And fear'st to die? famine is in thy
cheeks, Need and oppression starveth in
thine eyes, Contempt and beggary hangs upon
thy back; The world is not thy friend nor
the world's law; The world affords no law to
make thee rich; Then be not poor, but break
it, and take this.

APOTHECARY

My poverty, but not my will, consents.

ROMEO

I pay thy poverty, and not thy will.
Apothecary Put this in any liquid thing you
will, And drink it off; and, if you had the
strength Of twenty men, it would dispatch
you straight.

ROMEO

There is thy gold, worse poison to men's souls, Doing more murders in this loathsome world, Than these poor compounds that thou mayst not sell. I sell thee poison; thou hast sold me none. Farewell: buy food, and get thyself in flesh. Come, cordial and not poison, go with me To Juliet's grave; for there must I use thee.

Exeunt

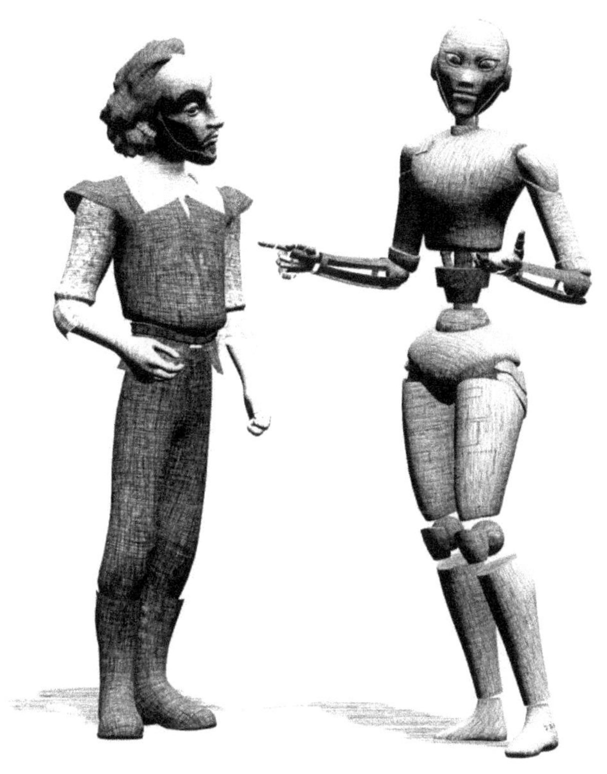

SCENE 2. FRIAR LAURENCE'S CELL.

Enter FRIAR JOHN

FRIAR JOHN
    Holy Franciscan friar! brother, ho!

Enter FRIAR LAURENCE

FRIAR LAURENCE
    This same should be the voice of Friar
    John. Welcome from Mantua: what says Romeo?
    Or, if his mind be writ, give me his
    letter.

FRIAR JOHN

Going to find a bare-foot brother out One of
our order, to associate me, Here in this
city visiting the sick, And finding him, the
searchers of the town, Suspecting that we
both were in a house Where the infectious
pestilence did reign, Seal'd up the doors,
and would not let us forth; So that my
speed to Mantua there was stay'd.

FRIAR LAURENCE

Who bare my letter, then, to Romeo?

FRIAR JOHN

I could not send it,--here it is again,—
Nor get a messenger to bring it thee, So
fearful were they of infection.

FRIAR LAURENCE

Unhappy fortune! by my brotherhood, The
letter was not nice but full of charge Of
dear import, and the neglecting it May do
much danger. Friar John, go hence; Get me
an iron crow, and bring it straight Unto my
cell.

FRIAR JOHN

Brother, I'll go and bring it thee.

Exit

FRIAR LAURENCE

Now must I to the monument alone; Within
three hours will fair Juliet wake: She will
beshrew me much that Romeo Hath had no
notice of these accidents; But I will write
again to Mantua, And keep her at my cell

till Romeo come; Poor living corse, closed
in a dead man's tomb!

Exit

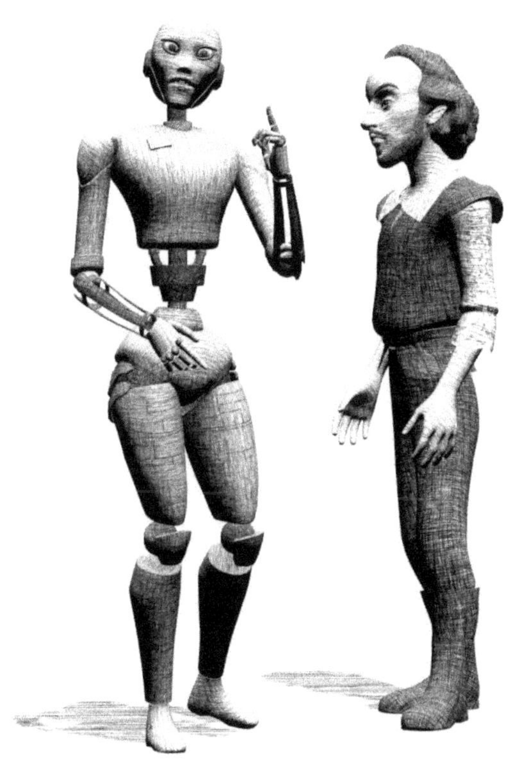

SCENE 3. A CHURCHYARD; IN IT A TOMB BELONGING TO THE CAPULETS.

Enter PARIS, and his Page bearing flowers and a torch

PARIS

> Give me thy torch, boy: hence, and stand
> aloof: Yet put it out, for I would not be
> seen. Under yond yew-trees lay thee all
> along, Holding thine ear close to the
> hollow ground; So shall no foot upon the
> churchyard tread, Being loose, unfirm, with
> digging up of graves, But thou shalt hear

it: whistle then to me, As signal that thou
hear'st something approach. Give me those
flowers. Do as I bid thee, go.

PAGE

(Aside)
I am almost afraid to stand alone Here in
the churchyard; yet I will adventure.

Retires

PARIS

Sweet flower, with flowers thy bridal bed I
strew,— O woe! thy canopy is dust and
stones;— Which with sweet water nightly I
will dew, Or, wanting that, with tears
distill'd by moans: The obsequies that I
for thee will keep Nightly shall be to
strew thy grave and weep.

The Page whistles

PARIS

The boy gives warning something doth
approach. What cursed foot wanders this way
to-night, To cross my obsequies and true
love's rite? What with a torch! muffle me,
night, awhile.

Retires

*Enter ROMEO and BALTHASAR, with a torch, mattock,
and a crow of iron.*

ROMEO

Give me that mattock and the wrenching
iron. Hold, take this letter; early in the
morning See thou deliver it to my lord and

father. Give me the light: upon thy life, I
charge thee, Whate'er thou hear'st or
seest, stand all aloof, And do not
interrupt me in my course. Why I descend
into this bed of death, Is partly to behold
my lady's face; But chiefly to take thence
from her dead finger A precious ring, a ring
that I must use In dear employment:
therefore hence, be gone: But if thou,
jealous, dost return to pry In what I
further shall intend to do, By heaven, I
will tear thee joint by joint And strew
this hungry churchyard with thy limbs: The
time and my intents are savage-wild, More
fierce and more inexorable far Than empty
tigers or the roaring sea.

BALTHASAR

I will be gone, sir, and not trouble you.

ROMEO

So shalt thou show me friendship. Take thou
that: Live, and be prosperous: and
farewell, good fellow.

BALTHASAR

(Aside)
For all this same, I'll hide me hereabout:
His looks I fear, and his intents I doubt.

Retires

ROMEO

Thou detestable maw, thou womb of death,
Gorged with the dearest morsel of the
earth, Thus I enforce thy rotten jaws to
open, And, in despite, I'll cram thee with
more food!

Opens the tomb

PARIS

> This is that banish'd haughty Montague,
> That murder'd my love's cousin, with which
> grief, It is supposed, the fair creature
> died; And here is come to do some villanous
> shame To the dead bodies: I will apprehend
> him.

Comes forward

PARIS

> Stop thy unhallow'd toil, vile Montague!
> Can vengeance be pursued further than
> death? Condemned villain, I do apprehend
> thee: Obey, and go with me; for thou must
> die.

ROMEO

> I must indeed; and therefore came I hither.
> Good gentle youth, tempt not a desperate
> man; Fly hence, and leave me: think upon
> these gone; Let them affright thee. I
> beseech thee, youth, Put not another sin
> upon my head, By urging me to fury: O, be
> gone! By heaven, I love thee better than
> myself; For I come hither arm'd against
> myself: Stay not, be gone; live, and
> hereafter say, A madman's mercy bade thee
> run away.

PARIS

> I do defy thy conjurations, And apprehend
> thee for a felon here.

ROMEO

Wilt thou provoke me? then have at thee,
boy!

They fight

PAGE

O Lord, they fight! I will go call the
watch.

Exit

PARIS

O, I am slain!

Falls

PARIS

If thou be merciful, Open the tomb, lay me
with Juliet.

Dies

ROMEO

In faith, I will. Let me peruse this face.
Mercutio's kinsman, noble County Paris!
What said my man, when my betossed soul Did
not attend him as we rode? I think He told
me Paris should have married Juliet: Said
he not so? or did I dream it so? Or am I
mad, hearing him talk of Juliet, To think
it was so? O, give me thy hand, One writ
with me in sour misfortune's book! I'll
bury thee in a triumphant grave; A grave? O
no! a lantern, slaughter'd youth, For here
lies Juliet, and her beauty makes This
vault a feasting presence full of light.

Death, lie thou there, by a dead man
interr'd.

Laying PARIS in the tomb

ROMEO

How oft when men are at the point of death
Have they been merry! which their keepers
call A lightning before death: O, how may I
Call this a lightning? O my love! my wife!
Death, that hath suck'd the honey of thy
breath, Hath had no power yet upon thy
beauty: Thou art not conquer'd; beauty's
ensign yet Is crimson in thy lips and in
thy cheeks, And death's pale flag is not
advanced there. Tybalt, liest thou there in
thy bloody sheet? O, what more favour can I
do to thee, Than with that hand that cut
thy youth in twain To sunder his that was
thine enemy? Forgive me, cousin! Ah, dear
Juliet, Why art thou yet so fair? shall I
believe That unsubstantial death is
amorous, And that the lean abhorred monster
keeps Thee here in dark to be his paramour?
For fear of that, I still will stay with
thee; And never from this palace of dim
night Depart again: here, here will I
remain With worms that are thy chamber-
maids; O, here Will I set up my everlasting
rest, And shake the yoke of inauspicious
stars From this world-wearied flesh. Eyes,
look your last! Arms, take your last
embrace! and, lips, O you The doors of
breath, seal with a righteous kiss A
dateless bargain to engrossing death! Come,
bitter conduct, come, unsavoury guide! Thou
desperate pilot, now at once run on The

dashing rocks thy sea-sick weary bark!
Here's to my love!

Drinks

ROMEO

O true apothecary! Thy drugs are quick.
Thus with a kiss I die.

Dies

Enter, at the other end of the churchyard, FRIAR LAURENCE, with a lantern, crow, and spade

FRIAR LAURENCE

Saint Francis be my speed! how oft to-night
Have my old feet stumbled at graves! Who's
there?

BALTHASAR

Here's one, a friend, and one that knows
you well.

FRIAR LAURENCE

Bliss be upon you! Tell me, good my friend,
What torch is yond, that vainly lends his
light To grubs and eyeless skulls? as I
discern, It burneth in the Capel's
monument.

BALTHASAR

It doth so, holy sir; and there's my
master, One that you love.

FRIAR LAURENCE

Who is it?

BALTHASAR

Romeo.

FRIAR LAURENCE

How long hath he been there?

BALTHASAR

Full half an hour.

FRIAR LAURENCE

Go with me to the vault.

BALTHASAR

I dare not, sir My master knows not but I am gone hence; And fearfully did menace me with death, If I did stay to look on his intents.

FRIAR LAURENCE

Stay, then; I'll go alone. Fear comes upon me: O, much I fear some ill unlucky thing.

BALTHASAR

As I did sleep under this yew-tree here, I dreamt my master and another fought, And that my master slew him.

FRIAR LAURENCE

Romeo!

Advances

FRIAR LAURENCE

Alack, alack, what blood is this, which stains The stony entrance of this sepulchre? What mean these masterless and gory swords To lie discolour'd by this place of peace?

Enters the tomb

FRIAR LAURENCE
Romeo! O, pale! Who else? what, Paris too?
And steep'd in blood? Ah, what an unkind
hour Is guilty of this lamentable chance!
The lady stirs.

JULIET wakes

JULIET
O comfortable friar! where is my lord? I do
remember well where I should be, And there
I am. Where is my Romeo?

Noise within

FRIAR LAURENCE
I hear some noise. Lady, come from that
nest Of death, contagion, and unnatural
sleep: A greater power than we can
contradict Hath thwarted our intents. Come,
come away. Thy husband in thy bosom there
lies dead; And Paris too. Come, I'll
dispose of thee Among a sisterhood of holy
nuns: Stay not to question, for the watch
is coming; Come, go, good Juliet,

Noise again

JULIET
I dare no longer stay.

JULIET
Go, get thee hence, for I will not away.

William Shakespeare

Exit FRIAR LAURENCE

JULIET
What's here? a cup, closed in my true love's hand? Poison, I see, hath been his timeless end: O churl! drunk all, and left no friendly drop To help me after? I will kiss thy lips; Haply some poison yet doth hang on them, To make die with a restorative.

Kisses him

JULIET
Thy lips are warm.

FIRST WATCHMAN
(Within)
Lead, boy: which way?

JULIET
Yea, noise? then I'll be brief. O happy dagger!

Snatching ROMEO's dagger

JULIET
This is thy sheath;

Stabs herself

JULIET
There rust, and let me die.
Falls on ROMEO's body, and dies

Enter WATCHMEN, with the Page of PARIS

PAGE

This is the place; there, where the torch doth burn.

FIRST WATCHMAN

The ground is bloody; search about the churchyard: Go, some of you, whoe'er you find attach. Pitiful sight! here lies the county slain, And Juliet bleeding, warm, and newly dead, Who here hath lain these two days buried. Go, tell the prince: run to the Capulets: Raise up the Montagues: some others search: We see the ground whereon these woes do lie; But the true ground of all these piteous woes We cannot without circumstance descry.

Re-enter some of the WATCHMEN, with BALTHASAR

SECOND WATCHMAN

Here's Romeo's man; we found him in the churchyard.

FIRST WATCHMAN

Hold him in safety, till the prince come hither.

Re-enter others of the WATCHMEN, with FRIAR LAURENCE

THIRD WATCHMAN

Here is a friar, that trembles, sighs and weeps: We took this mattock and this spade from him, As he was coming from this churchyard side.

FIRST WATCHMAN

A great suspicion: stay the friar too.

William Shakespeare

Enter the PRINCE and Attendants

PRINCE

What misadventure is so early up, That
calls our person from our morning's rest?

Enter CAPULET, LADY CAPULET, and others

CAPULET

What should it be, that they so shriek
abroad?

LADY CAPULET

The people in the street cry Romeo,Some
Juliet, and some Paris; and all run,With
open outcry toward our monument.

PRINCE

What fear is this which startles in our
ears?

FIRST WATCHMAN

Sovereign, here lies the County Paris
slain;And Romeo dead; and Juliet, dead
before,Warm and new kill'd.

PRINCE

Search, seek, and know how this foul murder
comes.

FIRST WATCHMAN

Here is a friar, and slaughter'd Romeo's
man; With instruments upon them, fit to open
These dead men's tombs.

CAPULET

O heavens! O wife, look how our daughter
bleeds! This dagger hath mista'en--for, lo,

his house Is empty on the back of
Montague,— And it mis-sheathed in my
daughter's bosom!

LADY CAPULET

O me! this sight of death is as a bell,
That warns my old age to a sepulchre.

Enter MONTAGUE and others

PRINCE

Come, Montague; for thou art early up, To
see thy son and heir more early down.

MONTAGUE

Alas, my liege, my wife is dead to-night;
Grief of my son's exile hath stopp'd her
breath: What further woe conspires against
mine age?

PRINCE

Look, and thou shalt see.

MONTAGUE

O thou untaught! what manners is in this?
To press before thy father to a grave?

PRINCE

Seal up the mouth of outrage for a while,
Till we can clear these ambiguities, And
know their spring, their head, their true
descent; And then will I be general of your
woes, And lead you even to death: meantime
forbear, And let mischance be slave to
patience. Bring forth the parties of
suspicion.

FRIAR LAURENCE

I am the greatest, able to do least, Yet
most suspected, as the time and place Doth
make against me of this direful murder; And
here I stand, both to impeach and purge
Myself condemned and myself excused.

PRINCE

Then say at once what thou dost know in
this.

FRIAR LAURENCE

I will be brief, for my short date of
breath Is not so long as is a tedious tale.
Romeo, there dead, was husband to that
Juliet; And she, there dead, that Romeo's
faithful wife: I married them; and their
stol'n marriage-day Was Tybalt's dooms-day,
whose untimely death Banish'd the new-made
bridegroom from the city, For whom, and not
for Tybalt, Juliet pined. You, to remove
that siege of grief from her, Betroth'd and
would have married her perforce To County
Paris: then comes she to me, And, with wild
looks, bid me devise some mean To rid her
from this second marriage, Or in my cell
there would she kill herself. Then gave I
her, so tutor'd by my art, A sleeping
potion; which so took effect As I intended,
for it wrought on her The form of death:
meantime I writ to Romeo, That he should
hither come as this dire night, To help to
take her from her borrow'd grave, Being the
time the potion's force should cease. But
he which bore my letter, Friar John, Was
stay'd by accident, and yesternight
Return'd my letter back. Then all alone At
the prefixed hour of her waking, Came I to

take her from her kindred's vault; Meaning
to keep her closely at my cell, Till I
conveniently could send to Romeo: But when
I came, some minute ere the time Of her
awaking, here untimely lay. The noble Paris
and true Romeo dead. She wakes; and I
entreated her come forth, And bear this
work of heaven with patience: But then a
noise did scare me from the tomb; And she,
too desperate, would not go with me, But,
as it seems, did violence on herself. All
this I know; and to the marriage Her nurse
is privy: and, if aught in this Miscarried
by my fault, let my old life Be sacrificed,
some hour before his time, Unto the rigour
of severest law.

PRINCE

We still have known thee for a holy man.
Where's Romeo's man? what can he say in
this?

BALTHASAR

I brought my master news of Juliet's death;
And then in post he came from Mantua To
this same place, to this same monument.
This letter he early bid me give his
father, And threatened me with death, going
in the vault, I departed not and left him
there.

PRINCE

Give me the letter; I will look on it.
Where is the county's page, that raised the
watch? Sirrah, what made your master in
this place?

PAGE

>   He came with flowers to strew his lady's
>   grave; And bid me stand aloof, and so I
>   did: Anon comes one with light to ope the
>   tomb; And by and by my master drew on him;
>   And then I ran away to call the watch.

PRINCE

>   This letter doth make good the friar's
>   words, Their course of love, the tidings of
>   her death: And here he writes that he did
>   buy a poison Of a poor 'pothecary, and
>   therewithal Came to this vault to die, and
>   lie with Juliet. Where be these enemies?
>   Capulet! Montague! See, what a scourge is
>   laid upon your hate, That heaven finds means
>   to kill your joys with love. And I for
>   winking at your discords too Have lost a
>   brace of kinsmen: all are punish'd.

CAPULET

>   O brother Montague, give me thy hand: This
>   is my daughter's jointure, for no more Can
>   I demand.

MONTAGUE

>   But I can give thee more: For I will raise
>   her statue in pure gold; That while Verona
>   by that name is known, There shall no figure
>   at such rate be set As that of true and
>   faithful Juliet.

CAPULET

>   As rich shall Romeo's by his lady's lie;
>   Poor sacrifices of our enmity!

PRINCE

A glooming peace this morning with it
brings; The sun, for sorrow, will not show
his head: Go hence, to have more talk of
these sad things; Some shall be pardon'd,
and some punished: For never was a story of
more woe Than this of Juliet and her Romeo.

Exeunt

End of Play

Thank you for enjoying **William Shakespeare's**
Romeo and Juliet in augmented reality!

Look for other titles at:

<u>livingpopups.com</u>

"I'll wait until it comes out in AR!"